CLEVELAND
BEER

CLEVELAND
BEER

HISTORY & REVIVAL
IN THE RUST BELT

LESLIE BASALLA AND PETER CHAKERIAN

AMERICAN PALATE

Published by American Palate
A Division of The History Press
Charleston, SC
www.historypress.net

Copyright © 2015 by Leslie Basalla and Peter Chakerian
All rights reserved

First published 2015

Manufactured in the United States

ISBN 978.1.46711.779.1

Library of Congress Control Number: 2015948354

CONTENTS

FOREWORD

Beer—you could say it was what Cleveland was founded on in the late 1700s. And it's again beer that, some two hundred years later, is fueling the renaissance of our fair city. Just as those early settlers brewed up a great new home on the shores of Lake Erie, modern day re-settlers are using beer and brewing to rebuild Cleveland's neighborhoods in this post-industrial frontier city.

What was shall be again.

Cleveland's renaissance has created vibrant, dense, walkable neighborhoods with locally brewed craft beer flowing everywhere, and the historic Ohio City neighborhood on the near west side is the epicenter. In 1988, Ohio City saw the opening of the state's first local craft brewery since Prohibition, Great Lakes Brewing Company. Nearly twenty years later, the neighborhood is home to dozens of restaurants, beer bars, wine bars, cafés, galleries and more. Leading the charge was a succession of craft breweries starting in 2011 with Market Garden Brewery, then Nano Brew Cleveland, Platform Brewery, Brick and Barrel Brewery and Winery and soon Hansa Brewery and Forest City Brewery.

The wider city and suburbs have gained their share of acclaimed breweries, with many serving as hubs for their own neighborhoods, and there seems to be no end in sight.

FOREWORD

Clevelanders are a fun-loving and broad-shouldered people, and they have had an affinity for local beer and the conviviality it brings to gatherings of family and friends since the city was founded.

And the beery best is yet to come…

Cheers and beers,
SAM MCNULTY
Owner, Market Garden Brewery and Nano Brew Cleveland

ACKNOWLEDGEMENTS

There are a great many people whose contributions and support made this book possible. We cannot begin to express our gratitude enough.

Leslie Basalla would like to thank:

Brian P. McCafferty for tolerating all the time I put into the research and writing of this book—time I could have been spending with him—and for and always being willing to listen when I needed encouragement.

My parents, Thomas and Mary Beth Basalla; my brothers, Greg and Nate; and my entire family.

Bob and Shelle Campbell, the former owners of the Cleveland Brew Bus, for bringing me into the business and inadvertently dropping the opportunity to write this book into my lap.

Carl Miller, for his inestimable scholarship on Cleveland brewing history and incredible generosity in sharing images from his collection.

Jenna Fournier for shooting a lovely author photo.

Bonnie Flinner and Prosperity Social Club for photos of their excellent collection of local breweriana.

The helpful staff at Cleveland Public Library.

John Bowen, for being the first person, way back when, to believe in me as a writer.

All of my service industry friends, past and present.

And last but absolutely not least, all of the incredibly devoted and passionate people working at Cleveland's craft breweries, especially Paul Benner, Shaun Yasaki, Ralph Sgro, Bill Reilly and Ken Wagenhouser of

ACKNOWLEDGEMENTS

Platform Beer Company; Janet and Jamie Hall, Tom Gray, Michael Zoscak and Ted Lipovan of Fat Heads; Matt and Kathy Chappel of Indigo Imp; Sam McNulty and the whole crew at Market Garden and Nano; Luke Purcell of Great Lakes; Karl Spiesman and Darrell Mikols of Brick and Barrel; and Jason Kallicragas, Andy Knecht and Ken Budney Jr. of the BottleHouse.

Peter Chakerian would like to thank:

Layne Anderson, the Beckwiths, Laura Watilo Blake, Marc Bona, Kelsey Brubaker, Susan Carroll, the Chakerians (all of them), Bruce Chamberlin, Cleveland Landmarks Press (Greg Deegan, Jim Toman, John Yasenosky), the Cook-Provost clan, Joe Crea, Brittyn DeWerth, Joe Dubbs, Eric and Cynthia Eakin, David Farkas, Michael Gallucci, Glenn Gamboa, David Giffels, the Giffords (all of them), Gray & Company, Kristen Hampshire, Annette and Joe Jones, Al Kaston, Glenn Kenny, Mandy Kizcek, Chuck Klosterman, Cheryl Kushner, Kenny and Tracy Larson and kids, Steven Liss, Janet Macoska, Eleanore McLaughlin, Chris McVetta, Vern Morrison, Kay Morrow, Thomas Mulready and Carol Hunt, John L. Nagy, Michael Norman, Eric Olsen, Susan Petrone, Karen Robinson, Connie Schultz, Jane Scott, Paula Schleis, Joseph Sheppa, Jim Szatkowski and Retta Kalcik, Claudia J. Taller, Sarah Toman, Douglas Trattner, Shelley Underwood and family, Carlo Wolff and Karen Sandstrom and Chuck Yarborough.

Special thanks to the Cleveland State University Digital Production Unit/ Cleveland Memory Project and all the fine, helpful folks at CSU's Michael Schwartz Library. None of this would have been possible without you.

INTRODUCTION

While I was in New Connecticut, I laid out a town on the bank of Lake Erie, which was called by my name, and I believe the child is now born that may live to see the place as large as Old Windham.
—Moses Cleaveland, 1796

When the city of Cleveland's founder arrived atop a high bluff at the mouth of the Cuyahoga River in July 1796, he could not possibly have conceived of the future size and prosperity of the village his surveyors were about to map out. His optimistic prediction that the town might surpass Windham, Connecticut, in population within a generation indeed came true. By 1837, Cleveland was a major commercial hub of the Great Lakes and boasted a population of 9,000 residents, quite a few more than Windham's 2,700.

By 1920, Cleveland was the fifth-largest city in the United States, boosted by a robust manufacturing industry. While steel was the city's best-known product, one of its best loved, especially by its own residents, was beer. Starting around the 1840s when an influx of German immigrants brought their taste for lager to Lake Erie's shores, the city has had a venerable tradition of brewing, and much the like the town itself, Cleveland's beer industry grew immensely with time.

Of course, since those heady days, the city's commercial landscape has changed considerably. Prohibition struck a nearly devastating blow to local brewing, just as the Great Depression shook the city's economy. The World

INTRODUCTION

War II years and immediate postwar period brought another heyday to Cleveland, both industrially and in the realm of brewing. But by the 1960s and '70s, as heavy manufacturing largely collapsed around the Great Lakes, earning the region the moniker of the "Rust Belt," brewing followed suit. Outcompeted by national brands and consolidated into nonexistence, Cleveland's legendary old breweries disappeared one by one, until, at last, in 1984, there were none.

But Cleveland is nothing if not resilient, and Clevelanders are fiercely proud of their city and its products, so it is no surprise that as local breweries have reestablished themselves, riding the rising tide of craft beer, the population has embraced them passionately. Great Lakes Brewing Company started the craft beer revolution in Cleveland in 1988, and many other breweries have established themselves in its wake. Of late, the city is experiencing a remarkable renaissance, fueled largely by small businesses. Craft beer has been a huge part of Cleveland's comeback, and there seems to be no end in sight to the local brewing scene's exponential growth, as new breweries seem to be opening or announced nearly monthly. It is with great pleasure and excitement that we chronicle the rise, fall and return of brewing here in the heart of the Rust Belt.

Chapter 1
WHISKEY AND TAVERNS IN THE WESTERN RESERVE

In 1796, when the shareholders of the Connecticut Land Company selected General Moses Cleaveland, a man with a reputation for being resourceful and brave, to lead an expedition to survey their newly acquired territory in the Western Reserve, the land would have been virtually unrecognizable to a modern-day Clevelander. Mostly covered by dense hardwood forests and populated by Native Americans, a handful of French and English fur traders and copious wildlife, it was a wild and remote place, hard to access.

Cleaveland's party set out from Schenectady, New York, that spring and reached the mouth of the Cuyahoga River on July 22. Impressed with the lay of the land, the clarity of the water and the quality timber to be found in the uplands, Cleaveland determined that the site would be well suited for a town. On August 26, Cleaveland's surveyors laid out the first maps of the city.

In the fall of 1796, most of the party returned to Connecticut. Moses Cleaveland himself never came back to the village that the members of the expedition named after him, but by 1797, a handful of hearty pioneers had settled in the town, and others began to populate the surrounding wilderness and neighboring townships.

CLEVELAND BEER

FRONTIER LIBATIONS

Life in the early days of the Western Reserve was a hardscrabble existence. Most settlers lived in relative isolation, building log cabins on scattered homesteads and clearing small portions of the forest to farm. Most of the towns in the area consisted of only a small number of dwellings. Cleveland's initial population after the expedition of 1796 was a mere four. The next year it swelled to fifteen but dropped to seven by 1800, due to the residents scattering to other towns around the locality.

Roads between the area villages and homesteads—if they existed at all—were narrow tracks built along the routes of old Indian trails, riddled with roots and ruts. Given the difficulty of travel and trade, it is little wonder that early settlers in the Western Reserve probably did not consume a great deal of beer. Grain was scarce and could more efficiently be put to use as whiskey, the preferred intoxicant and staple beverage of the frontier. Whiskey was more potent and, hence, much more portable than beer. Traders did a brisk business in whiskey sales, and early distillers made a tidy profit converting the local farmers' grain harvests into alcohol.

Zerah Hawley, an itinerant doctor from Connecticut who worked in northeastern Ohio through the years of 1820–21, reported, "The productions are, wheat, rye, all of which or nearly all, is distilled into whiskey, which (with the exception of water), is the principal drink of the inhabitants, as there are but few orchards from which cider is yet made, and foreign spirits or wine is hardly known here." According to Hawley, the locals also used large quantities of corn to make whiskey.

If settlers had any beer at all, it would have been made in the home, probably by the lady of the house, using whatever fermentable ingredients were available, including sugar, bran, molasses, pumpkins, spruce boughs and even green pea shells. The majority of the settlers were New Englanders by birth, primarily from Connecticut and mostly of British descent. They would have brewed ales—generally "small" or "table" beer—low-alcohol brews intended for immediate consumption. On a rare occasion, they might have had enough grain or other fermentables on hand to make a stronger beer "for keeping," but it is more likely that such supplies would have been distilled into whiskey instead.

Early Cleveland Taverns

Despite its tiny population at the time, David and Gilman Bryant established Cleveland's first commercial distillery in 1800 on the Cuyahoga River at the foot of Superior Street. It was capable of making two quarts of whiskey a day, using water drawn from a nearby spring. The Bryants had no shortage of customers between the white settlers and the local Native Americans. Two years later, early residents Lorenzo Carter and Amos Spafford bought the city's first tavern licenses and presumably kept a stock of the little distillery's product.

Carter's home was already well established as the center of local society, having been the site of the town's first public ball and its first wedding. "It served as a hotel for strangers, and as a variety shop of hunting supplies," according to local historian Harvey Rice, whose 1885 book, *Sketches of the Western Reserve*, contains a colorful chapter devoted to Carter.

The tavern became a destination for residents as well as all visitors passing through the village. It was located on the north side of Superior Street near Water Street (present-day West Ninth Street). Carter died in 1814, but the tavern remained open under the ownership of a Phineas Shepherd.

First settler Lorenzo Carter's cabin in the Cleveland Flats. Carter was one of the city's first tavern keepers. *Photo by Leslie Basalla.*

The history and location of Spafford's Tavern is a little more difficult to pinpoint, but existing documents suggest it was located near the foot of Superior, on Vineyard Street (around modern-day Merwin Avenue), close to what is now the eastern base of the Veteran's Memorial (Detroit-Superior) Bridge. Part of the confusion stems from the fact that the tavern changed hands several times. Sometime between 1810 and 1815, another famous early resident, George Wallace, purchased it and renamed it the Wallace House.

Wallace had already been operating another tavern for a few years on the south side of Superior near present-day West Third Street. That establishment he sold to Michael Spangler, who changed the name to Spangler's Inn.

Noble Merwin purchased the Wallace House in 1822, tore down the original structure and replaced it with a new two-story frame building, to which he applied a much-grander name: the Mansion House. The Mansion House was a favorite local landmark and the site of many important functions until it burned down in 1835. The Wallace House name is memorialized today at Market Garden Brewery, the owners of which christened their Wallace Tavern Scotch Ale in its honor.

In 1815, Phineas Mowry built a tavern on Public Square, on the site of what is now the Renaissance Cleveland Hotel. This particular location has been occupied by a tavern or hotel ever since.

The Franklin House, also located on the busy thoroughfare that Superior Avenue was becoming by that time, opened in 1826. By the time owner Philo Scovill opened its doors, regular stagecoach service between Cleveland and other major cities, including Erie and Pittsburgh and Columbus and Cincinnati, had increased demand for lodging. The Franklin House had a reputation for cleanliness and good food.

These early taverns were similar in structure to the frame houses of the settlers. Most socializing and drinking were conducted in a main living room, which generally did not have a bar. If there was a bar, it was not furnished with stools and was simply a barrier between the thirsty patrons and the liquor behind it. In *Cleveland: The Making of a City*, author William Ganson Rose describes Carter's tavern thusly: "A spacious living room, kitchen and two bedrooms constituted the first floor, with a large chimney in the center. Several rooms and an attic were upstairs. With lumber from Detroit, a local carpenter built furniture for the first hotel in Cleveland."

It is likely that these early tavern keepers were also the city's first commercial brewers, cooking up small batches of ale and porter in their

Hubach's Tavern, one of Cleveland's typical early saloons. *Courtesy of Carl H. Miller.*

own kitchens, and selling it for on-premise consumption, as well as to neighboring households.

In addition to being meeting places, the taverns also served as rooming houses for travelers or newly arriving settlers.

Canal Days

Cleveland's growth was very slow in its early years, primarily owing to the fact that the town was difficult to access for trade purposes. Overland travel remained slow and laborious. A small shipping industry had been established on the Great Lakes, but Cleveland lacked a proper harbor, and unlike today, boats could not access the Cuyahoga River to bring goods to the settlers and businesses on its banks.

The mouth of the Cuyahoga River, as residents now know it, is, in fact man-made, having been excavated in 1825 to create a direct connection to Lake Erie and alleviate the swampy conditions of the surrounding land. The original river mouth was about three hundred yards to the west and choked by a sandbar, causing the water to pool around the western end of present-day Whiskey Island. The stagnant water and rotting vegetation (as well as any other effluent from the settlement) was a breeding ground for bacteria and mosquitoes, and early residents were frequently ill as a result of the foul conditions.

Many early settlers in Cleveland, frustrated by the constant battles with sickness, moved to other towns on higher ground, particularly Newburgh, where they enjoyed better health. Indeed, in its early years, Cleveland was in danger of losing its population as a result of the pestilential conditions.

A Scottish traveler, John Melish, who visited the Western Reserve in 1811 to survey its suitability for immigration, thought highly of Lake Erie and of Cleveland's potential but observed the poor health of the residents he met. "The people looked pale, sickly, and dejected," he wrote, "I learned that they had been greatly afflicted with a very severe sickness this season. It was periodical, they said, and generally fever and ague; but this season it had been worse than usual and accompanied with some very severe cases of bilious fever. I found that this had proved a complete check upon the improvement of Cleveland, which, though dignified with the name of a city remained a paltry village containing a few houses only."

Melish presciently suggested that cutting a new channel from river to lake at the base of the bluff could relieve the little town's problems. He wrote, "Should these circumstances be attended to and succeed, the result would make Cleveland a very healthy, as it certainly is a very beautiful place…The subject deserves legislative attention."

The issue finally received state funding in 1825. After the initial excavation of the river mouth and the subsequent addition of a second pier in 1827, the Cuyahoga became navigable to schooners plying the lakes, and the village began to grow and prosper. It was also in 1825 that Cleveland was selected to be the northern terminus of the Ohio and Erie Canal, which, along with the opening of the Erie Canal in New York, would connect the city to a much larger network of commerce.

The new shipping networks sped up transportation of goods and allowed for beer to be shipped to Cleveland in quantity from more established eastern cities, particularly Philadelphia and later Pittsburgh. The beer also occasionally arrived from other Great Lakes ports. The *Cleveland Herald* devoted extensive coverage to the arrival of twenty-five barrels of beer from Detroit in one 1829 issue. Any large shipment of "foreign beer" was a cause for excitement.

Supplied by those sporadic ale shipments, as well as their own homebrew, an increasing number of taverns, saloons and general stores appeared as the town began to boom.

Cleveland resident and early newspaper printer David Hudson Jr.'s diary of 1825 mentions purchasing a glass of "small beer" at a grocery for two cents. Hudson's diary also mentions the increasing number of European immigrants arriving in town at the time. His opinion of the Irish, who arrived in droves to excavate the Ohio and Erie Canal, was unfavorable.

Hudson's view of the new immigrants, who initially numbered around two hundred, was typical. The authors of *Irish Americans and their Communities of Cleveland* describe them as "rough and tumble, mannerless men, who seemed interested only in obtaining the bare necessities of life and drinking the saloons along the riverfront dry."

While whiskey was reportedly the preferred drink of the canal workers, they undoubtedly consumed a good quantity of ale in the thirteen saloons that sprang up in their principal settlement, the aptly named Whiskey Island.

If the digging of the canal brought population growth, its official opening in 1827 swelled the city's populace even more, as new businesses and industries were established. Census numbers from this period bear out the town's rapidly accelerating growth. Cleveland's population in 1825 was 500. By 1831, it had more than doubled to 1,100. By January 1834, it had reached 3,323 residents, and by November of that year, it was up to 4,250. When Julius Bolivar McCabe published the city's first directory in 1837, he quoted the population as being more than 9,000.

The demand for beer was growing with the population, and the city's first commercial breweries finally opened in the 1830s. McCabe's directory lists two, under the heading of "Manufactories," but does not give their names—one was probably that of Elijah Willey, who briefly operated an ale brewery along a creek called Walworth Run, near the present-day Animal Protective League. Very few details are known about Willey's brewery, but it is presumed that it did not exist for very long. The other brewery mentioned in McCabe's directory was almost certainly the Cleveland Brewery.

Chapter 2

CLEVELAND'S EARLY ALE BREWERIES

THE CLEVELAND BREWERY

The earliest documented commercial brewery in Cleveland was the Cleveland Brewery, which opened in 1832, on Canal Street on the East Bank of the river. The first owners were Robert Bennett and Dr. Samuel J. Weldon. Like most of the early breweries in the city, the Cleveland Brewery's main products were ale, porter and stout—styles that traced their heritage back to England. Ale was lighter in body and color than the other two, which, like their modern counterparts, were dark brown to black. Hops were probably used when available. Other classifications of beer, more nebulous by modern style standards, were also available, including small beer, table beer, common beer and strong ale—the names described the ale's relative alcoholic strength.

The Cleveland Brewery went through a rather complicated series of changes of ownership over its lifetime. Weldon sold his interest in the company within a year of opening, while Bennett added a malt house. Brothers Joseph and Richard Hawley purchased the brewery in 1834, but by 1837, Joseph dropped out, and brewer Herrick Childs stepped in. By 1839, Childs was the sole proprietor and the brewery was reportedly producing 1,600 barrels a year. The Hawley family was back in the picture a year later, when a Thomas Hawley and his son-in-law, John Hawley Cooke, leased it. Hawley and company pioneered bottling in Cleveland, offering bottled ale and porter. Childs returned to ownership in 1843 and replaced the old brewery with a new brick building, possibly as a result of a fire.

A print advertisement for Ive's, "Brewer, Maltster, Hop Dealer," including nods to its porter, brown stout and Old Beeswing Ale. *Courtesy of Carl H. Miller.*

In 1847, Herrick sold out to Samuel C. Ives, who operated the company as Ives' Cleveland Brewery until his death in 1856. During Ives's tenure as owner, the brewery's output expanded to seven thousand to eight thousand barrels per year. The brewmaster, an aptly named John C. Brewer, was considered one of the "best brewers in the country," according to an account in the *Cleveland Leader*.

After Ives's death, the ownership of the company passed to his fourteen-year-old daughter, Eliza. Eliza's guardians leased the company to a series of operators for the next six years. Her husband, Frank D. Stone, took over management in 1862. The brewery was destroyed by fire in 1865, with arson by "Confederate emissaries" the reported cause.

Spring Street Brewery/The Hughes Brewery

Brewer John M. Hughes arrived in Cleveland from Albany, New York, in 1847 and went to work for Truman Downer, who, the year before, had opened the Spring Street Brewery. The brewery was located on Spring Street (West

Print advertisement for John M. Hughes Ale touting its health benefits. *Courtesy of Carl H. Miller.*

Tenth), between Main and St. Clair Avenues. By 1850, Downer decided to leave Cleveland for Chicago. He and his business partner, Thomas F. Wyman, sold the brewery, excluding the adjacent malt house, to Hughes for $3,200. The new company was named the John M. Hughes Brewery.

Hughes's tenure as owner started rather inauspiciously, as a fire completely destroyed the building just six months after he bought it. Hughes quickly rebuilt and soon was successful enough to require a major expansion. In 1857, he constructed a new brewery and malt house on West Street between Merwin Avenue and Vineyard Street, facing the Ohio and Erie Canal. By 1858, the brewery was churning out ten thousand barrels of beer a year and employed twenty men. The malt house collapsed in a freak accident later that year, but employees were able to recover most of the twelve thousand bushels of grain it contained. Two local malting companies, owned by John B. Smith and Louis Umbstaetter, generously stored the grain until the building could be replaced.

Hughes's specialties included India pale ale, cream ale, porter, stock ale and something called champagne ale. Print advertisements for the brews touted their health benefits, depicting a well-dressed man declaring, "I drink Hughes Ale," beside a ragged derelict saying, "I don't."

The brewery's success made a wealthy man of Hughes and allowed his wife, Eliza, to become a charitable benefactor to the Cleveland Protestant Orphan Asylum.

Upon Hughes's death in 1871, ownership of the brewery passed to Eliza. His nephew Levi F. Ives (no relation to Samuel Ives), oversaw operations. Hughes's brother Arthur took over ownership in 1888 and incorporated as the Hughes Brewing Company, with Ives continuing as superintendent.

By 1894, demand for ale had decreased dramatically, as most drinkers abandoned it in favor of the lager beers brewed by the city's German immigrants. The brewery's output, by then, had diminished to a mere 1,500 barrels a year, so it was not marked a great loss when the J.&A. McKenchie Brewing Company of Canandaigua, New York, bought the building for use as a distribution center. McKenchie operated the facility until 1898, when local brewer Hugh Spencer took it over and resumed brewing ale. Spencer's brewery lasted only until 1901, and when it closed its doors, ale brewing in Cleveland was as good as over.

Incidentally, two of the brewmasters who worked for Hughes over the years, Carl Gehring and Leonard Schlather, would go on to fame and wealth as owners of two of the city's largest and most prosperous lager breweries.

Other Cleveland Ale Breweries

Samuel Ives and John Hughes were not the only successful owners in the heyday of Cleveland's ale breweries. They had a number of other competitors over the years between 1832 and the early 1900s.

The Forest City Brewery opened in 1839 on Seneca Street (West Third) and produced primarily stock ale under the auspices of Charles C. Rogers, an Irishman who ran the company until 1871. A series of subsequent owners continued to brew ale there, until selling out to Carling and Company of London, Ontario, in 1880. Now named the London Brewery, Carling moved the plant to a new location four years later and produced ales at that site until 1898, when the facility became part of the Cleveland and Sandusky Brewing Company combine, representing the only ale brewery in the otherwise lager-producing trust.

The Eagle Brewery was another early entrant into the ale market, opening in the early 1840s at 32 Michigan Street near Seneca (now covered by the Terminal Tower complex). It burned to the ground in December 1845 but was rebuilt and continued operating until 1869.

A different Forest City Brewery operated from around 1850 to 1883. It was located on Irving Street (East Twenty-fifth) and produced around 3,500 barrels a year its peak. While it started as an ale brewery exclusively, Forest City began brewing lagers in the 1870s.

The Lloyd and Keys Cleveland City Brewery began business in 1859 on St. Clair at West Ninth. It remained in business until 1909, later than most of the other ale breweries in town, only shutting down due to the failing health of owner Daniel H. Keys. The Lloyd and Keys name is better known in Cleveland than many of its larger competitors thanks to an old painted advertisement preserved on one of the exterior walls of Great Lakes Brewing Company's pub. Guests enjoying a beer on the patio or in the beer garden can admire the sign, touting the medicinal benefits of the brewery's "old stock and Kennett ales on draught."

Trade and Prosperity

Thanks to Cleveland's position on the Ohio and Erie Canal, its access to Great Lakes shipping vessels and, by the mid-1850s, to a fast-growing network of railroads, beer from the city's breweries was enjoyed both here and all around the region. About one-fifth of the 53,500 barrels of beer produced in the city in 1867, for example, was shipped out of Cleveland via lake freighter, railroad and canal boat, according to a statement of trade and commerce published by city hall.

The city's growth as a trade center made it a popular destination for many of those seeking their fortunes. By the census of 1850, the city's population had reached 17,034. Even the editor of the *Cincinnati Gazette* was impressed by Cleveland's prospects, calling it "the most desirable town in the 'Great West' to live in." Quite a few of the incoming residents were German immigrants, who brought with them a taste for lager beer and the skill required to brew it. Soon, quite a few would open their own breweries and change the face of beer in Cleveland forever.

Chapter 3

GERMAN BREWERS AND THEIR LAGER BEER

LAGER BEER

Beer is generally classified into two great families—ale and lager. The differences between the two boil down to one element—yeast. Ales are fermented with a yeast species called *Saccharomyces cerevisiae*, while lagers employ a different strain, *Saccharomyces pastorianus*. The term "lager" comes from the German verb *lagern*, which means "to store," because lagers are matured after fermentation for several weeks to several months, usually under very cold conditions. During lagering, the yeast absorbs many flavor and aroma compounds, leaving behind a clear, clean-tasting beer.

According to *The Oxford Companion to Beer*, "For virtually all of human history until roughly the mid-1800s, and unbeknown to the brewer and drinker, beers became either ales or lagers more or less by happenstance, depending on the ambient temperature and overall climate."

In temperate conditions, ale yeasts are able to accomplish fermentation before the lager yeasts are able to grow. However, in winter, ale yeasts would go dormant, allowing the lager yeasts to ferment batches of beer. Because bacteria are also mostly dormant in winter, beers brewed in the colder months were less likely to become infected and go sour.

The authors of the *Companion* note, "This fact did not escape the attention of brewers in Central Europe during the Middle Ages. For this reason, Duke Albrecht V of Bavaria decreed in 1553 that henceforth in his realm, all beer brewing had to stop between April 23 and September 29. It was with this decree—perhaps much underappreciated even by beer historians—that Bavaria, with its cold winters in the foothills of the Alps, was moved firmly into the development of lager beer. From then on, by necessity, any beer style developments in Bavaria had to be in lagers."

Lager did not catch on outside of Central and Northern Europe for several centuries. Ales remained dominant in Great Britain and hence became the preferred beers of the English colonists in America and their descendants, as well as the many immigrants who arrived later from Ireland, Scotland and Wales.

By the 1840s and '50s, however, many Germans were making their way to the United States, bringing with them a distinctive beer drinking and brewing culture. "For them," writes Randy Mosher in *Tasting Beer*, "a world without the joys of a few lagers in the garden on a Sunday afternoon was just unthinkable, and as they were men of ambition and skill, they set about rebuilding their beer culture here, pretty much from scratch."

Early German settlers in Cleveland were mostly descendants of families who had arrived in Pennsylvania, New York and Maryland prior to the Revolutionary War. German immigration to Cleveland began in earnest in the 1830s and increased dramatically, spurred by political unrest and crop failures at home, in the late 1840s.

With the influx of immigrants came demand for lager and places to drink it. William Richter opened the first lager bar in Cleveland on Ontario Street. Jacob Mueller, founder of *Wachter am Erie*, a German-language newspaper, lauded its arrival as a boon to the German community. "The new institution was greeted by Teutons, both old and young, dedicated to good drink, particularly recent immigrants who could find no enjoyment in the usual drinks, such as 'Present Use,' 'Stock Ale,' and 'Ginger Pop.' To have lager beer from the tap in the land of hard liquor, what German nature, friendly to drinking could not have felt the pull of home?"

Richter's establishment was quickly followed by many more lager saloons. The *Cleveland City Directory of 1857–58* listed more than seventy-five of them. Regardless of the popularity of lager bars, though, the true homes of beer drinking for Cleveland's German families were the city's outdoor beer gardens.

CLEVELAND BEER

Cleveland Beer Gardens

For Germans arriving in America, preservation of their language and culture was important. In Cleveland, as in other cities, they established German-language newspapers, singing societies, drama clubs, *turnverein* (or gymnastic) clubs and, almost always, beer gardens. Outdoor beer gardens are an integral part of beer culture in Bavaria, and the local immigrants sought to replicate the experience here. Beer gardens were not just drinking venues—they were also social and cultural centers and featured spaces for musical or theater performances, picnicking areas, pavilions for dancing and recreational spaces for sports. Whole families would while away Sunday afternoons in the gardens, enjoying the peaceful setting and, of course, quite a bit of lager.

Cleveland's earliest beer gardens, such as Volk's Garden and Trinkner's Garden, were located right in the heart of the city, but in order to facilitate a more pastoral atmosphere (and later to avoid laws forbidding Sunday alcohol sales), the longest-running and most popular gardens were located on the outskirts of town along Willson Street (East Fifty-fifth).

The year 1862 saw the opening of Haltnorth's Garden at Willson Street and Woodland and its neighbor, Lied's Garden at Willson and Outhwaite.

Described by Rose, Haltnorth's Garden was "a wooded lot, nearly half a block square [that] contained a pond crossed by a rustic bridge and a garden that was a favored picnic spot." It also featured a museum, a bowling alley, a rifle range and a huge concert hall, which contained a saloon and two restaurants. The open-air theater was where most of the entertainment took place, with performances by popular light opera companies and the Cleveland Philharmonic Orchestra.

Lied's Garden was of similar size and was open to the public on Sundays only. Owner Balthasar Lied and his family lived on the property, and he acted as the park's official host and master of ceremonies, even after he leased it to outside management in 1883.

A little to the north, on Willson Street and St. Clair Avenue, was Paul Kindsvater's Garden, which opened in 1866. Prior to opening the garden, Kindsvater owned a lager saloon and was a partner in a lager brewery. It was probably not a coincidence that he also was a director of the St. Clair Railroad, a streetcar line that conveniently carried residents from the center city right to his doors.

While the gardens were generally family-friendly locales and instrumental in the establishment of many local cultural institutions, such as the Cleveland

28

Orchestra, the patrons could get rowdy. Lager-fueled brawls erupted from time to time—frequently enough, in fact, that city officials made attempts to stop streetcars from running to the gardens on Sundays.

German immigrants found these efforts, along with the Sunday temperance laws enacted in the 1870s, to be examples of a stifling Yankee prudery common to the greater local population. Wrote Mueller, "The puritanic spirit which virtually dominated life here would rather have darkened the sun than tolerate cheerful festivities or celebrations on Sunday."

EARLY LAGER BREWERIES

The years between 1846 and 1870 saw many lager brewers establish themselves in Cleveland and slowly come to dominate the local market. By 1870, about two-thirds of the beer brewed annually in Cleveland was lager. The 1870s were truly the golden age of lager brewing locally, with as many as twenty-six breweries in operation. The trend toward lager, though, started slowly.

The Stumpf Brewery

Recent German immigrants Michael and Martin Stumpf opened the earliest known lager brewery in Cleveland in 1846. It is not known if the brothers brewed lager immediately on opening or only after having established themselves by brewing and selling ale. What is known is that the brewery, which was located on Lake Street (Lakeside Avenue) between Muirson (East Twelfth) and Canfield (East Thirteenth) Streets, never grew particularly large and primarily peddled its wares to nearby lager saloons. The brewery's production peaked in 1875 at about 1,100 barrels per year.

Martin Stumpf parted ways with his sibling in 1850 to establish a new brewery on his own, a block to the east. Michael Stumpf continued to run the business alone in spite of a fire in 1857 that leveled the building. He rebuilt and had the brewery back in business by 1860. Faced with diminishing sales, he closed the plant in 1882 and converted it into a home, where his family continued to reside.

CLEVELAND BEER

Lion/Jacob Mall Brewery

The original name of the brewery that Martin Stumpf established on Hamilton Street between Canfield and Muirson Streets in 1850 is unknown, but it went on, through several changes in ownership, to be one of the longest-surviving breweries in Cleveland.

The first change of hands came in 1859, when Stumpf sold the works to Jacob Mall and Paul Kindsvater. Mall was a German-trained brewmaster, and Kindsvater owned a popular lager saloon on St. Clair (he later owned Kindsvater's Garden). The two called their business the Lion Brewery and expanded production rapidly. By 1870, demand for their beer outstripped the plant's capacity. They built a new facility on Davenport Avenue, on a site previously owned by Martin Stumpf. The new brewery overlooked the lake, and it is likely that lagering tunnels were carved directly into the face of the bluff below, allowing easy access to ice in the winter.

Kindsvater left the partnership in 1871. Mall pressed on, building the business on the back of its flagship product, Mall's Crystal Lager. The company incorporated as the Jacob Mall Brewery in 1889. By 1891, when Mall died and passed management on to his son-in-law, Gustav Kaercher, production had reached ten thousand barrels a year.

The brewery continued to grow throughout the 1890s, despite periods of recession and ever-increasing competition from other local breweries. An entirely new, four-story plant was erected in 1896, increasing capacity to thirty thousand barrels.

Kaercher sold the company a year later to George Gund, who would take it to dizzying heights of success under his own name.

The Schmidt and Hoffman/Cleveland Brewery

The Stumpf brothers were the first men to brew lager in Cleveland, but it was two other German immigrants, C.W. Schmidt and Robert Hoffman, who proved it could be a successful commercial venture. The pair launched their brewery in 1852 in an unlikely location—the sparsely settled township of East Cleveland. Although the site, at the corner of Ansel and Hough Avenues, is now just blocks from the thriving museum district of University Circle, it was, at the time, mostly forest. While far from the city center, Schmidt and Hoffman's five-acre parcel was situated on Doan Brook, which provided clean water and included a pond, from which ice could be harvested in the winter.

The staff of the Cleveland Brewing Company. *Courtesy of Carl H. Miller.*

Production at the plant started modestly but grew quickly, from a mere seven hundred barrels in 1852 to seven thousand by the 1870s. Hoffman died in 1882 and Schmidt in 1884. Their sons Louis Hoffman and Carl Schmidt took over ownership and were joined in 1887 by Ernst Mueller. With Mueller on board, the firm changed its name to the Cleveland Brewery and underwent a rapid expansion from ten thousand barrels in 1887 to forty thousand just ten years later. Over time, the Mueller family came to dominate management at the old brewery, with Ernst's cousins and brothers occupying most of the executive positions.

In 1898, the Cleveland Brewery was one of nine breweries in the city, and two in Sandusky, to merge into a combine called the Cleveland and Sandusky Brewing Company. Mueller eventually became president of the new company and continued to expand the plant under the new management structure. The plant stopped producing beer in 1919 at the onset of Prohibition and never returned to brewing.

Other Lager Breweries

A number of additional lager breweries existed in Cleveland between 1850 and 1900. Most were very small and could not compete with the local brewing behemoths that began their rise in the late 1850s and 1860s, and most remained in business for less than thirty years.

These breweries included the John A. Bishop brewery (1852–91), the Mack Brothers Brewery (1852–74), the John Dangeleisen Brewery (1856–74), the Michael Lucas Brewery (late 1850s–74), the Weidenkopf/Whitlock Brewery (1858–74), the Stumpf/Davies/Gavagan Brewery (1863–90s), the Jacob Wagner Brewery (1864–73), the Wittlinger/Porter Brewery (1866–77), the Joseph Koestle Brewery (1867–82), the Phillip Griebel Brewery (1868–82), the August Burkhardt Brewery (1868–80), the Henry Hoffman Brewery (1871–81) and the J.M. Mack Brewery (1874–82). A number of very small Weiss beer breweries also came and went over the years, making small quantities of traditional Bavarian wheat beer, but most never grew enough to qualify as more than large homebrewing operations.

Chapter 4
THE RISE OF THE BEER BARONS AND THE GOLDEN AGE OF BREWING IN CLEVELAND

While the Stumpf Brothers and Jacob Mall pioneered lager brewing in Cleveland, and Schmidt, Hoffman and Mueller capitalized on its growing popularity, it was the men who began opening breweries in the late 1850s and '60s that made their brands household names and, in turn, amassed vast fortunes from the sparkling, golden beverages that flowed from their works.

Men like Carl Gehring, Isaac Leisy, Leonard Schlather and Andrew Oppman established some of the largest and most successful breweries the city would ever see and lived resplendent lives in stately mansions, often situated on the grounds of their breweries. These beer barons took advantage of new technologies like steam power, mechanized bottling lines and artificial refrigeration to supply ever-increasing quantities of beer to a growing population whose thirst rarely seemed to be satisfied.

The economic climate in the city at the time was perfect for these ambitious businessmen. Buoyed by expanding railroad networks and massive manufacturing industries, Cleveland flourished and continued to attract waves of immigrants and entrepreneurs seeking to build their fortunes. The city's population reached 43,417 in 1860. The Civil War years brought banking crises to the city, but its industrial growth continued, providing the beer barons with an expanding populace to enjoy their products.

THE C.E. GEHRING BREWING COMPANY

Carl Ernst Gehring was already a well-established figure in Cleveland's brewing industry in 1857, when he opened his own brewery at the junction of Pearl (West Twenty-fifth) and Brainard (later renamed Gehring) Streets. Originally from Goeppingen, Württemberg, Germany, where he apprenticed at a brewery from the age of fourteen, Gehring arrived in Cleveland in 1848 and quickly found employment, first at the Eagle Brewery and later at the Spring Street Brewery. He stayed on at the latter as brewmaster after John M. Hughes took over ownership in 1850. Gehring took advantage of a lapse in production at the Hughes Brewery in 1857, when it expanded, to strike out on his own.

In its earliest days, Gehring's Brewing Company produced ale and porter alongside lager. Gehring himself was the only employee and turned out only 1,800 barrels in his first year of business. As the German population increased and demand for lager grew, the brewery grew as well, reaching an annual production of 12,000 barrels by 1874.

The brewery's footprint expanded by 1876 to cover several blocks between Pearl, Brainard and Freeman Streets—an area now encompassing the Market Square shopping plaza at West Twenty-fifth Street and Lorain Avenue and stretching eastward to the present day West Twenty-fifth Street Rapid Transit Station. The massive plant included a 155-barrel brew kettle—the largest in the city at the time—plus thirty-six fermenters, two icehouses, malting facilities and an underground warren of lagering tunnels.

Six delivery teams carried beer from the brewery to Cleveland's saloons and beer gardens—the horses and wagons were a common sight on city streets. The beer itself was becoming a common sight outside of Cleveland, as it was shipped to Pennsylvania, New York and West Virginia. The brewery was a true family business, with Gehring's sons and son-in-law occupying various positions.

Business continued to boom into the 1880s—probably the most prosperous decade for Cleveland's German brewers. A new brewhouse in 1885 nearly doubled capacity, and production reached sixty-eight thousand barrels by 1888. Gehring parlayed his brewery's success into other ventures. He served on city council, was Cleveland's police commissioner in 1875 and was president of the Forest City Bank. Gehring died in 1893, one year after incorporating the brewery as the C.E. Gehring Brewing Company. The brewery was the third-largest in the city at the time.

An illustration of the Gehring Brewery. *Courtesy of Carl H. Miller.*

His sons took over ownership after his death and continued to expand the business, but by 1898, it had joined the Cleveland and Sandusky Brewing Company combine. It was the largest brewery involved in the merger, producing ninety thousand barrels in 1901. The combine closed the plant in 1918, as Prohibition loomed, and the entire complex was razed a year later. None of the buildings remain.

THE L. SCHLATHER BREWING COMPANY

The details of Leonard Schlather's life almost mirror those of his neighbor and eventual competitor, Carl Gehring. The two hailed from the same German town and grew up together. Gehring arrived in Cleveland a few years ahead of Schlather, but the latter's career path, once in the city, followed a similar trajectory. Schlather settled first in Altoona, Pennsylvania, and obtained his first brewery job there. He came to Cleveland three years later, possibly at Gehring's urging, and joined the staff of the Hughes Brewery. By 1857, on Gehring's heels, he left the company to form his own brewery.

Like Gehring's, Schlather's operation started modestly—his two-story frame building at York (West Twenty-eighth) and Bridge Streets housed an almost comically small four-barrel brewing system. Within five years, however, his business had increased enough to allow him to purchase a

Portrait of Leonard Schlather. *Courtesy of Carl H. Miller.*

parcel of land one block south, at York and Carroll Streets, and greatly expand the plant. By 1874, the brewery was producing eighteen thousand barrels per year, and by 1878, Schlather needed to replace the entire facility in order to meet demand.

Schlather's new brewery was a commanding, ornate structure of brick and stone, standing four stories tall. It was designed by local architect Andrew Mitermiler, who was behind the impressive, castle-like appearance of many of Cleveland's largest breweries. The distinctive building became a local landmark and was featured in much of the company's print advertising and promotional materials. Its large scale allowed production to increase to twenty-seven thousand barrels by 1879.

In addition to the brewing facilities themselves, the complex comprised a number of satellite buildings, including a garage for delivery wagons and stables for the horses. Carroll Street was the first in the city to be paved with bricks, making the task of pulling heavily loaded wagons much easier in rainy, muddy weather. Horse teams delivered most of the brewery's beer throughout the city, but some of it was distributed to other areas of Ohio. Schlather owned a chain of saloons along the Ohio River, all of which carried his products. Some beer made it as far as Pittsburgh.

Schlather and his family resided, after 1881, in a stately Italianate house across York Street from the brewery. The house burned in 1970. St. Ignatius High School's practice field now occupies the site.

The brewery incorporated in 1884 as the L. Schlather Brewing Company and put out fifty thousand barrels that year. The company produced numerous varieties of beer, including a pilsner, a Munich lager and a Kulmbacher (black lager), as well as Standard and Export lagers.

The imposing Schlather Brewing building, which once stood at West Twenty-eighth Street and Carroll Avenue. *Courtesy of Cleveland Public Library.*

John Schneider was brewmaster, and under his guidance, output increased to seventy thousand barrels by the mid-1890s and around ninety thousand barrels in 1900, making Schlather the city's second-largest brewery. It was during this period that the company ventured into bottled beer, adding a bottling plant on the south side of Carroll Avenue.

By the turn of the century, Schlather was in his sixties and considering retirement. Like Gehring, he was involved in many other civic and financial pursuits. He was active in the Cleveland Chamber of Commerce and the Western Reserve Historical Society and, with his second wife, Sophie, traveled the world extensively. Unlike Gehring, however, Schlather had no sons to pass the brewery on to, only five daughters. The culture and tradition of the time would not allow him to hand over the company to a woman, so in 1902, he sold the brewery into the Cleveland and Sandusky Brewing combine. It became the largest facility in the company, which also took over ownership of Schlather's more than sixty saloons. This was a huge boost for the combine and helped it to dominate beer sales in Cleveland and the region for the next seventeen years.

Schlather himself passed away in 1918. The Cleveland and Sandusky combine continued to use the brewery through Prohibition to manufacture soft drinks. By 1933, however, operations were moved to more modern facilities, and every building except the bottling plant was torn down. Dave's Supermarket now occupies the brewery site. Great Lakes Brewing Company bought the bottling building in 1997; it now houses the company's brewhouse and bottling line.

Isaac Leisy Brewing Company

The man who would eventually own the largest and most famous brewery in Cleveland, Isaac Leisy, did not arrive in the city until 1873, but the brewery that he took over had been in business since 1858. The brewery on Vega Avenue at the corner of Fulton Road commenced operations under owner Jacob Mueller. Frederick Haltnorth, better known as the proprietor of Haltnorth's Garden, bought the brewery in 1864 and began increasing its capacity. The plant was turning out around twelve thousand barrels a year in 1873, when Cleveland hosted the Thirteenth Annual Brewers Congress.

Among the many brewers from around the country who attended the conference was Isaac Leisy. Leisy, who had immigrated to the United States with his entire extended family in 1855, was a part owner of the Leisy and Brothers Union Brewery in Keokuk, Iowa. Impressed with Cleveland's booming economy and burgeoning European immigrant population, Leisy viewed a move to Cleveland as an opportunity to succeed on a much grander scale than he could have back in Iowa. Less than a month later, he and his brothers August and Henry purchased Haltnorth's brewery and began one of the longest-lasting and best-remembered brewing legacies in the city's history.

Because Isaac held the largest share of the company, the brewery bore his name, but all three brothers ran Isaac Leisy and Company with zeal and assertiveness. Cleveland's extensive shipping connections via railroad allowed the brothers to easily distribute their beer throughout the region, and they quickly pushed into markets outside the city. By 1876, they had established a distribution depot in Pittsburgh, to which Henry relocated. Two years later, sensing the potential of bottled beer well before most of their peers, the Leisys opened a bottling plant across the street from the brewery. The brewery's production around this time was between eighteen thousand and twenty-four thousand barrels annually, making it the city's second-largest brewery.

Early exterior shot of the Leisy Brewing Company on Vega Avenue. *Courtesy of Carl H. Miller.*

Cleaning the beer vats at the Leisy brewery. *Courtesy of Carl H. Miller.*

A close-up of the King Gambrinus statue once located at Leisy Brewing Company. Plans are underway to restore the "patron of beer drinkers" effigy to its former glory and place it in Ohio City's Market Square Park. *Courtesy of Special Collections, Cleveland State University Archives.*

In 1882, Henry and August left the company and moved to Nebraska to run a farm, selling their shares to Isaac. It has been suggested that the two, who were raised in a rural part of Germany, could not get used to city life and might not have been able to reconcile their Mennonite upbringing with profiting from the sale of alcohol. With Isaac at the helm, the company continued to expand, and over the next several years, he transformed the Vega Avenue brewing complex into a visually stunning landmark.

Early Leisy delivery wagon. *Courtesy of Carl H. Miller.*

The metamorphosis began in 1883, when a new stockhouse for cold aging of beer (designed by brewery architect Andrew Mitermiler) was built. By the end of 1884, a new malt house and brewhouse, all in the same extravagant, Victorian style, were in place. The roofline of the new brewery sported a life-size statue of King Gambrinus, a legendary German-culture hero and patron of beer and brewing. After a hailstorm knocked it down in 1909, the statue was placed in the brewery yard.

The complex extended well beyond the brewing and malting facilities. There was a stable for the nearly 250 horses that pulled the brewery's delivery wagons and shops for the many auxiliary tradesmen whose products were needed to keep the brewery operating—blacksmiths and harness-makers kept the horses outfitted, and a cooperage provided wooden beer barrels. There was even a woodworking shop on site to build bar fixtures for the company's many affiliated saloons.

The park-like grounds featured a pond, gardens, walking paths, two greenhouses and a brownstone mansion, built in 1892, where the beer baron himself lived. Isaac's son Otto also had a house on the premises, a Victorian that had previously been Haltnorth's home. By the time Isaac's impressive

The ornate Isaac Leisy mansion located on Vega Avenue, right beside the Leisy brewery. *Courtesy of Special Collections, Cleveland State University Archives.*

residence was complete, the brewery was the largest in the city, with annual output reaching eighty thousand barrels.

Isaac Leisy did not get to enjoy his mansion or his brewery's success for long. He passed away in 1892, leaving management of the company to Otto. Otto was twenty-nine at the time of his father's death and had grown up observing the growth of the brewery. He faced challenges almost immediately upon taking over ownership. Competition among Cleveland brewers was intense at the time, as many had expanded too rapidly and were fighting for product placement in saloons and favor among home consumers.

The nation underwent a financial panic in 1893 as well, with eight thousand businesses closing and 150 banks collapsing over six months. Cleveland, overall, weathered the storm, but the economic disaster only increased the competition among brewers and ultimately pushed many toward consolidation. When nine Cleveland breweries and two in Sandusky merged to create the Cleveland and Sandusky Brewing Company in 1898, Otto Leisy was steadfast in his refusal to join.

A horse-drawn Leisy Brewing Company beer delivery wagon shows two drivers pulling barrels of beer to their next destination. *Courtesy of Special Collections, Cleveland State University Archives.*

The younger Leisy's defiance seemingly paid off. In 1898, the brewery produced 100,000 barrels, and by 1913, the figure was triple that at 300,000 barrels. Like many other Cleveland beer barons before him, Leisy diversified his interests, investing in many other industries and ventures including the Forest City Railway, woolen mills in Cleveland and Ashtabula and a number of banks. He was director of the Lincoln Savings and Banking Company and vice-president of the Pearl Street Savings and Trust Company.

One of the original Leisy Brewing Company buildings on Vega Avenue. The complex included the brewing plant, bottling plant and shops for assorted trades, as well as gardens, greenhouses, walking paths and the owners' mansions. *Courtesy of Special Collections, Cleveland State University Archives.*

Like his father, Otto Leisy passed away rather young, dying at age fifty-one in 1914, just as the forces that would lead to national Prohibition were causing a slump in beer consumption.

Those who helped steward the company over the next few years—Otto's sister Amanda Corlett, who served as vice-president, and cousin Hugo Leisy, who was secretary and treasurer—focused on the bottling side of operations, predicting that household beer consumption was on the rise in the face of anti-saloon sentiment. A new bottling plant was erected in 1915, and by 1917, more than 30 percent of the brewery's output was being sold in bottles.

The year before Prohibition took effect, 1918, was Leisy's biggest year, with production peaking at 565,493 barrels. A very small amount of that production was accounted for by a new, nonalcoholic malt beverage called Bevera, which the family hoped would carry the business through the dry years. Given Cleveland's easy access to bootlegged beer and spirits from Canada, however, Bevera and similar beer substitutes simply never caught on. Leisy's plant limped on, producing a variety of soft drinks until 1923, when the family finally shuttered the works and poured six thousand barrels of Bevera into the sewer.

Ultimately, though, Leisy was one of the few local breweries to survive Prohibition, thanks to the family's many other financial interests and company's familiar and well-regarded presence in the community. When the company recommenced brewing in 1934, demand for its beer far outstripped its capacity, and Leisy would go on to regain its place as a locally beloved household name.

THE ANDREW W. OPPMAN/PHOENIX BREWERY

To say that Andrew W. Oppman lead a remarkable life, both before and after establishing his successful Cleveland brewery, would be a vast understatement. Originally from Bavaria and already apprenticed as a brewer, Oppman arrived in America in 1863 at the age of nineteen. He made his way to St. Louis and found a brewery job but quickly became bored and joined several friends headed to Kansas to establish a new town. The group was attacked by bandits, and a suddenly penniless Oppman joined the U.S. Army, serving in a cavalry unit that delivered ammunition and supplies to forts in the West.

His army stint only intensified his hunger for adventure, and in 1866, he took off on horseback for an eight-month journey to California. In San Francisco, a friend introduced him to a steamship captain, who hired him as a steward, and Oppman set sail across the Pacific. The restless young man did not care for life on the high seas, however, preferring to see the world and visit new ports of call. He joined the crew of a coastal steamship upon his return and made his way to Panama, where he crossed the isthmus on foot and boarded a ship that would eventually return him to the East Coast.

Finally satisfied that he had seen enough adventure, Oppman briefly worked for a brewery in New York before taking up the position of brewmaster at the Mueller Brothers Brewery in Chicago. Oppman would have happily remained there but for the Great Chicago Fire of 1871. Unemployed and broke in a devastated city, Oppman traveled on again, this time making his way to Cincinnati, where he joined a brewery supply company. A sales trip took him to Cleveland, where he met Frederick Haltnorth, who offered to make him brewmaster at his Vega Avenue Brewery. Aware of Cleveland's good economic prospects, Oppman accepted the job.

Ever restless and ambitious, Oppman did not stay long with Haltnorth. Only a few months after his arrival in Cleveland, he struck out on his own and bought Adam Schumann's brewery at Columbus and Willey Streets.

The brewery had been in operation since 1867 and was a small frame structure, producing only about 2,500 barrels annually. Growth was slow at first, but Oppman persisted and innovated as he went. A natural problem-solver, he devised new machines and equipment to expedite the brewing and packaging process, including a mechanized mash tun and a device that moved kegs from one floor of the brewery to another. By 1884, he had increased capacity tenfold and his brewery was the fifth-largest in the city. The brewery incorporated in 1887 as the Oppman Brewing Company.

On the Fourth of July in 1889, possibly sparked by errant fireworks, the brewery caught fire. The loss was nearly total, but Oppman quickly rebuilt, replacing the old plant with an ornate new brewhouse. Although the new facility would produce fifty thousand barrels within a decade, Oppman did not stick around to oversee its success. Like many of his fellow beer barons, he became involved in real estate. He sold his share of the brewery in 1891 and went on to develop a residential complex at West Boulevard and Madison Avenue that came to be called Oppman Terrace. Oppman Terrace still stands, although it is now called Boulevard Terrace, and is in use as affordable housing units.

The brewery's remaining shareholders rechristened the firm the Phoenix Brewing Company—a reference to its rise from the ashes just a few years before. Sales remained high, but by 1898, the Phoenix Brewing Company, like so many others, joined the Cleveland and Sandusky Brewing Company. In 1902, the combine closed the nearby Baehr brewery and moved its production to the Phoenix brewery, which was larger and had more modern equipment. The facility operated for the next six years as the Baehr-Phoenix branch of the combine but was shut down in 1908 as management looked to further consolidate brewing operations. The brewery never reopened. The Red Line Rapid Transit tracks run through what was the brewery site.

Chapter 5
COMPETITION AND CONSOLIDATION

The 1870s, '80s and '90s were days of expansion and optimism for Cleveland's breweries and a prosperous period for the beer barons, but their success was constantly at risk. As the local market became ever more crowded, brewers found themselves in fierce competition for consumers' attention and money. Worse still, national brands were emerging and entering the city, adding another, often well-funded layer of competition.

Brewers used different tactics to maintain customer loyalty. Many relied heavily on saloon business and supplied tavern owners with ornate fixtures, draft systems and other supplies or took care of expensive licensing fees in exchange for those establishments selling their products exclusively. Most breweries also directly owned saloons. The city was scattered with these "tied houses," and sometimes the same crossroads or block would feature two or three bars hawking different breweries' libations. Companies also turned to bottled beer and appealed to home consumers, hoping to make their beverages household staples, purchased weekly alongside other essentials by the city's housewives.

Some, like the Cleveland Brewery's Ernst Mueller, Gehring and Oppman, eventually came to the conclusion that the best hope against both their local competition and the national brewers was to consolidate. They were among the nine Cleveland breweries and two in Sandusky that eventually comprised the Cleveland and Sandusky Brewing Company. The others that joined have their own histories.

THE STOPPEL/COLUMBIA BREWERY

Joseph Stoppel arrived in Cleveland in 1848 and opened a saloon and distillery. Noting the rising popularity of lager beer, he began brewing in 1859, launching J. Stoppel and Co.'s Belle View Brewery on Canal and Ohio Streets in the Flats. The growing company was incorporated in 1869 as Stoppel's Actien Brewery. "Actien" is a German term indicating a business owned jointly by stockholders. Despite early success, with production reaching seven thousand barrels, Stoppel decided to return to Germany in 1872 and sold the brewery to J. Kraus and Company.

The new owners were not very good businessmen and defaulted on their mortgage by 1877, forcing a reluctant Stoppel to return from Europe and re-purchase the brewery in a public auction. After stabilizing operations, Stoppel again left the country, handing over management of the brewery to his sons Omar and Alphonso in 1882. The brothers improved and expanded the company, adding a new plant on Commercial Street and adopting new vacuum fermenting techniques that sped up the fermentation process and drastically decreased the risk of the beer spoiling.

Alphonso died in 1891, and a new group of investors bought the brewery, renaming it the Columbia Brewing Company. Production reached twenty thousand barrels by 1894. In 1898, the brewery was sold into the Cleveland and Sandusky Brewing Company. It remained in operation, producing about thirty-five thousand barrels a year, until the advent of Prohibition, when it was torn down.

THE BAEHR BREWERY

Jacob Baehr's journey in America took several unexpected turns before landing him in a brewing career in Cleveland. Baehr came to the United States from Heidelberg, Germany, in 1850 and settled in New York City, where he worked as a cooper. He did not stay there long before coming to Cleveland and establishing his own cooperage. By 1857, though, he left the city for Keokuk, Iowa, where he joined friend and fellow Mennonite John Leisy as a partner in the Leisy and Brothers Union Brewery. Not satisfied with the rural lifestyle, Baehr returned to Cleveland in 1866 and established his own lager brewery at the corner of Pearl (West Twenty-fifth) and Church Streets.

It did not take long for the plant, which also housed a saloon, to reach an annual production of three thousand barrels. Baehr's religious convictions led him to run an exceptionally disciplined operation—he would only employ men who regularly attended church, and he would not sell beer to anyone who drank in excess.

Baehr did not live to enjoy his brewery's success for long. He died in 1873, and the company passed into the capable hands of his widow, Magdalena, who, for the previous seven years, had run the saloon. Mrs. Jacob Baehr's Brewery, as she called it, expanded under her guidance. As sales increased, she upgraded the plant, adding a new brewhouse and stock house, as well as improved kegging facilities. She and her ten children resided on the brewery's top floor. Over time, her sons became involved in the operation—Emil served as brewmaster, while Herman was manager. By 1894, the Baehr Brewery was producing fifteen thousand barrels of six different styles of beer; that number had increased to twenty-five thousand by 1898, when Magdalena sold the company into the Cleveland and Sandusky Brewing combine.

Herman Baehr initially served on the combine's board of directors but eventually moved into banking, first with the Forest City Savings and Trust Company and later with the Cleveland Trust Company. He was elected mayor of Cleveland in 1910 and served a two-year term.

The old Baehr Brewery building remains completely intact. A real estate development company, the Foran Group, owns the building and plans to convert it into condominiums and apartments.

THE GEORGE MUTH/STAR BREWERY

The brewery that George Muth purchased in 1868 had been established a year earlier by Gottfried Reindl on what appeared to be an ideal site. Located on Buckley Street near Burton Street (West Forty-first), it sat on a hill above Walworth Run, a creek that, at the time, was still a source of clean water for brewing. The hillside allowed for easy digging of lagering tunnels, and a pond on the premises supplied ice. Reindl was better at site selection than he was at business, though, and defaulted on both of the mortgages he took out to build the brewery. Muth did not have any brewing experience when he purchased the company at public auction, but he and his brother Matthias jumped into the business regardless.

Matthias hanged himself three years later for unknown reasons. The coroner ruled it a case of "temporary insanity." After getting over his brother's suicide, Muth brought his son George V. Muth into the operation. By the time the elder Muth passed away in 1881, production at the brewery had increased to about 4,500 barrels a year.

In 1885, George V. Muth built a new three-story brick plant and renamed the company the Star Brewery. A traditional six-pointed brewer's star had always appeared on Muth's kegs. After contracting a case of blood poisoning that necessitated the amputation of one of his feet in 1895, though, Muth sold the company to brewers John M. Leicht and Carl A. Strangmann of Alexandria, Virginia. The two incorporated the next year as the Star Brewing Company. By 1898, the facility was producing about thirteen thousand barrels annually but was nevertheless among the first to join in the Cleveland and Sandusky combine. Leicht became vice-president of the new company, and the brewery continued to operate until 1913. The property was later sold and the brewery razed. No evidence of it remains today.

THE SCHNEIDER/UNION BREWERY

Christian Schneider was the third businessman in just two years to take ownership of the brewery at Train Avenue and Ash (West Forty-seventh) Street when he purchased it in 1872. Born in Bavaria, Schneider was a cooper and maltster who arrived in Cleveland in 1840.

He operated the brewery well below its eleven-thousand-barrel capacity for about a decade, typically only producing four thousand barrels annually. His son, John, joined the business in 1880 and took over nine years later when the elder Schneider retired.

The brewery was struck by lightning in 1891, and the resulting fire completely destroyed the plant. The loss was only partially covered by insurance, and although Schneider rebuilt, the business failed to recover. A new group of investors, which included two of Schneider's sons-in-law, took over in 1895 and renamed the facility the Union Brewing Company. The brewery's production never exceeded five thousand barrels under the new owners, making it one of the smallest in the city and a natural candidate for consolidation into the Cleveland and Sandusky merger. The combine used the brewery until 1902 and then sold the building. It later was home to the Bowman Ice Cream Company.

The building is still standing, but expansions by subsequent owners have rendered the original architecture almost unrecognizable.

THE BOHEMIAN BREWING COMPANY

Originally established as the William Aenis Brewery on Columbus Street in 1877, the brewery that would eventually become the Bohemian Brewing Company changed hands several times after relocating to Pearl Street and Vega Avenues in 1879. One of the owners was Bohemian immigrant Wenzl Medlin, who would go on to found the Pilsener Brewing Company.

In 1889, Medlin sold the brewery to a group of employees that included plant supervisor Simon Fishel. Fishel quickly worked his way into ownership and expanded the operation, eventually increasing its capacity to twenty-five thousand barrels by 1894. The company joined the Cleveland and Sandusky brewing combine at its inception in 1898, and Fishel joined its board of directors. His association with the combine would prove to be complicated and controversial over the ensuing years.

THE CLEVELAND AND SANDUSKY BREWING COMPANY

As the 1890s dawned, competition among Cleveland's breweries was intensifying, but it was far from the only factor that led to nine of them and two from Sandusky consolidating into a single entity.

The economic climate was changing—a recession in 1893 and 1894 caused beer consumption nationwide to drop by 1 million barrels. German immigration had slowed, meaning fewer new lager drinkers were reaching American shores. Many breweries were already overburdened with debt, having expanded too rapidly in the 1880s. Capacity exceeded demand.

Cleveland's brewers had considered a large-scale merger in 1892 and again in 1895, but in the former case, Isaac Leisy flatly refused to participate; it was his son and heir, Otto, who sunk the second proposal. As the decade drew to a close, new pressures made the idea of a combine more attractive.

In 1898, the federal tax on beer was increased from one dollar per barrel to two dollars in an effort to fund the Spanish-American War. Brewers passed the cost on to saloon owners, who in turn passed it to customers.

The tax proved disastrous for the beer business, as consumers responded by purchasing 1 million fewer barrels of beer over the ensuing year.

Trusts and mergers were forming in many industries, including among breweries. While some were mutual agreements, others were forced on brewers by outside investors. This was the case in cities like Baltimore, Chicago and Detroit, where British capital groups bought up as many breweries in each town as they could and combined them into single companies. This phenomenon is probably what ultimately shook Cleveland's brewers into action. Reportedly, British investors had approached Leisy, Schlather, Gehring, Stoppel and Oppman with purchase offers well in excess of their breweries' actual market values.

While most of the brewers were somewhat reluctant to consolidate, they all agreed that a merger of their own design would be preferable to having one foisted on them. In 1897, the Cleveland Brewers Association contracted a Philadelphia-based broker, John P. Persch, to obtain financing for and oversee the merger. By February 1898, the Cleveland and Sandusky Brewing Company was formed, with nine Cleveland breweries—Baehr, Barrett, Bohemian, Cleveland, Columbia, Gehring, Phoenix, Star and Union joining.

The Barrett Brewery was the only ale brewery in the combine. It had evolved from the old London Brewery, which owned the rights to produce Canadian brewing firm Carling's ales, stouts and porters stateside. Distributors Barrett and Barrett of Chicago acquired the brewery in 1891, renaming it in the process. Its capacity was around 150,000 barrels when it joined the combine.

The two Sandusky breweries were Kuebeler and Stang, which had already merged three years before into the Kuebeler and Stang Malting Company.

The brewery owners received cash for the sale of their properties, as well as stock in the new company, and once operations commenced, it was the brewers who were in charge. The management consisted of president F.W. Gehring, first vice-president Jacob Kuebeler, second vice-president Ernst Mueller and secretary/treasurer William Chapman. The board of directors included Herman Baehr, Henry Boehmke of the Phoenix Brewery, Emil Joseph of the Columbia Brewery, John Leicht of the Star Brewery, Simon Fishel and Frank Stang.

The stated purpose of the new company was "overcoming the evils of a ruinous competition," but competition between the combine and the city's handful of independent breweries remained intense and peppered with accusations of unfair business practices on both sides. The independents

A print ad for the Cleveland and Sandusky Brewing Company, featuring portraits of its board of directors and illustrations of its facilities. *Courtesy of Carl H. Miller.*

accused the combine of underselling them and luring saloon owners away. The Ohio Attorney General's office investigated the combine for violating the state's antitrust statutes in 1899 but eventually dropped the case.

Rumors that the combine had designs on encompassing breweries in all of Ohio's major cities circulated from time to time as well. While the combine did occasionally buy out additional breweries, like Schlather, which it acquired in 1902, the tales were unfounded. Regardless, the conglomerate was highly successful in its initial years, with the combined capacity of the breweries allowing it to nearly dominate local sales.

Although it closed or consolidated several facilities in Cleveland during its early years, the combine did open one new facility in 1904, the Lorain Brewery. By including Kuebeler and Stang in the merger, the company had gained control of one of the most popular beer brands in the western half of the region, Crystal Rock Beer. The plant was needed to produce enough Crystal Rock to supply the market all the way to Toledo. The brand became very popular in Cleveland as well and was marketed extensively toward women.

THE FISHEL BREWERY

With its executive offices and board of directors occupied by so many strong-willed, proud businessmen, it is perhaps not surprising that personality conflicts developed within the Cleveland and Sandusky Brewing Company. The most heated dispute was between Simon Fishel and Ernst Mueller. No single insult or point of contention seems to have set off the feud, but by 1904, it had intensified to the point that Fishel resigned his position as general manager of the combine and left the board of directors.

By early 1905, Fishel had already established a new brewery on East Fifty-fifth Street at Grand Avenue. The impressive five-story building housed one of the most modern brewing operations in the city and quickly began churning out barrels of Fishel $500 Bond Beer. The brew had a unique marketing gimmick—a promise from Fishel, whose signature appeared on the bottles, that the beer contained no "injurious substitutes" to the finest natural ingredients and a guarantee of $500 to anyone who could prove that promise false. The beer's name was later changed to $500 Gold Bond Beer and finally just Gold Bond Beer.

Between this novel promotion and Fishel's aggressive efforts to woo saloon owners, production at the brewery reached fifty-four thousand barrels within its first year, making it Cleveland's third-largest independent brewery. This did not escape the notice of Fishel's former colleagues in the combine, who began to consider absorbing the new brewery into the company. In March 1907, the Cleveland and Sandusky Brewing Company bought the Fishel Brewery for $850,000—an exorbitant sum of money to some members of the management. As part of the deal, Fishel was installed as president of the combine, and Mueller was ousted. While Mueller had voted in favor of the purchase, the other members of the board had conveniently neglected to inform him that he would lose his job as a result. It is believed that there was a faction within the management that wanted Mueller removed because of his disapproval, a few months earlier, of an attempt to purchase the Standard Brewing Company.

Mueller, for his part, recovered from his unceremonious departure. Within a year, he had purchased the Beltz Brewery, which he renamed the Cleveland Home Brewing Company. It would become one of the combine's fiercest competitors.

THE FISHEL YEARS

In the initial years following the acquisition of the Fishel Brewing Company, the Cleveland and Sandusky combine struggled financially. The high purchase price had, in fact, nearly bankrupted the company. By 1910, however, the combine had recovered and was again turning a profit. In addition to the highly popular Crystal Rock Beer, it now had Fishel's Gold Bond in its lineup, as well as other top sellers, such as Schlather Pilsner and Starlight and Carling's Ale and Porter. The company streamlined operations by closing the Baehr-Phoenix Plant in 1908, the Bohemian plant in 1911 and the Star plant in 1913. Sales throughout this period were steady at about 500,000 barrels per year.

As it became more and more apparent that Prohibition was inevitable, the company continued to shut down plants. In 1918, when Ohio passed a statewide Prohibition bill that was to take effect the next year, the combine shuttered the Columbia, Gehring, Kuebeler and Lorain facilities. The Fishel, Schlather and Stang plants remained open as the dry years commenced, producing near beer and other soft drinks. Only the Fishel and Stang plants would survive to reopen after repeal.

HISTORY & REVIVAL IN THE RUST BELT

Cleveland's Independent Breweries

Not every brewery in Cleveland succumbed to the appeal of joining the Cleveland and Sandusky Brewing Company. Alongside the stalwart Leisy, a number of established breweries stood their ground and continued to compete with the conglomerate. Following the turn of the century, a few new brewing concerns emerged and thrived as well, holding firmly to their share of the hearts and minds of local consumers. Some of these, like the Diebolt Brewing Company, closed at the onset of Prohibition, never to resume business. Others would not only survive Prohibition but also return as some of the city's greatest and best-loved brands post-1933.

The Diebolt Brewing Company

The brewing plant that Anthony J. Diebolt took over in 1891 had been in business, albeit never particularly successfully, since 1856. Its first owners established it as an ale brewery, and it changed ownership many times over the years until 1874, when Carl Seyler purchased it and added lager to its brewing repertoire, quickly increasing annual production from two thousand barrels to six thousand.

Diebolt arrived in Cleveland from his native Buffalo in 1887 and, after working for about a year at the Bohemian Brewing Company, purchased a share of ownership in the brewery at Pittsburgh Avenue and Jackson (East Twenty-seventh) Street from Seyler's successor, Louis Lezius. By 1891, Diebolt was the sole owner of the brewery and quickly went about expanding.

The plant's flagship beer was Diebolt's White Seal. By 1898, the brewery was producing twenty thousand barrels a year, and within nine years, that figure had increased to eighty thousand. By 1912, the facility had grown into a four-acre complex of six buildings, each featuring castle-like façades. The main buildings surrounded a central courtyard, while the horse stables were located across Jackson Street.

As anti-saloon agitation increased, the company shifted its focus to home sales of beer. A new bottling plant was constructed in 1915. Diebolt and his brothers, Joseph and Mattias, also launched an auxiliary business in 1908—the Cleveland Hygeia Ice Company. Ice produced by the brewery's machines was shipped

Illustration of the Diebolt Brewing Plant. *Courtesy of Carl H. Miller.*

out via rail lines located directly behind the plant. By 1911, ice production and storage accounted for a third of the facility's footprint.

Ice, along with the brothers' real estate holdings, helped get the company through the first years of Prohibition. Its beer substitute, Perlex Beverage, however, was not successful, and the plant ceased all beverage production by 1923.

The Diebolt brothers lost most of their property to the Van Sweringen family, who developed the Terminal Tower complex. The main buildings were demolished in 1928. Railroad and RTA Rapid Transit tracks leading into Tower City now cover the better part of the site. The stables survived until 1979 but were finally taken down to make way for the Orange Avenue Post Office.

THE PILSENER BREWING COMPANY

Pilsner beer, the light, crisp golden lager style to which most major American beer brands can trace their lineage, was originally developed in the town of Plzen, Bohemia, in what is now the Czech Republic. It makes sense, therefore, that the founder of Cleveland's Pilsener Brewing Company, had hometown roots in Plzen and learned the trade under that town's legendary brewmasters.

Wenzl Medlin emigrated from Bohemia to the United States in 1866 at the age of seventeen. Twenty years later, he arrived in Cleveland and spent a brief tenure as owner and brewmaster of the Bohemian Brewing Company. After selling out to Simon Fishel (who later merged Bohemian into the Cleveland and Sandusky combine), Medlin established a new brewery in 1893. Named the Medlin Pilsener Brewing Company, it stood at the corner of Clark Avenue and Gordon (West Sixty-fifth) Street.

A photo of Pilsener Brewing Company's enormous brew kettle. *Courtesy of Cleveland Public Library.*

Medlin was a fine brewer but a poor businessman—the new company was bankrupt within two years, and its president, Vaclav Humel, took over ownership, changing its name to the Pilsener Brewing Company. Medlin continued as brewmaster. Once recovered from its initial stumbles, the company grew rapidly from only six thousand barrels in 1894 to sixteen thousand the following year. By 1898, production hit twenty-six thousand barrels. By 1901, burgeoning sales enabled the company to build a new five-story brewhouse. Auxiliary buildings, including stables and a boiler house, soon followed.

The brewery's flagship was known as Extra Pilsener Beer but would become much more famous over time under the mysterious moniker P.O.C. The three letters began appearing on bottles as a slogan in 1907, one year after the growing brewery established a bottling works. By 1914, P.O.C. became the beer's brand name and trademark. The company remained intentionally vague about what the letters stood for, even sponsoring a P.O.C. guessing contest (although never awarding a winner) in 1915. The consensus among consumers was that the letters were short for Pride of Cleveland. The beer was truly a Cleveland brand—it was not marketed outside of the metropolitan area.

Despite its limited distribution, Pilsener continued to expand, adding a new three-story building on Clark Avenue in 1915 to house the company's offices and expanded bottling line. The new building also included a rathskeller, kitchen and assembly hall. A garage was added next door for delivery vehicles and wagons. Locals dubbed the sprawling complex "Pilsener Square," and the company offered public tours of its clean and modern facilities upon opening.

Like many other local breweries, Pilsener took up brewing near beer when Prohibition began in 1919. That, along with sales and home delivery of coal and ice, allowed it to survive the dry years relatively intact. It would be first local brewery to successfully resume beer making after repeal.

THE GUND BREWING COMPANY

When owner Gustav Kaercher greatly expanded the works at the well-established Jacob Mall Brewing Company in 1896, the modern, four-story facility caught the eye of businessman George F. Gund. Son of John Gund, a successful LaCrosse, Wisconsin brewer, George Gund had recently returned

A German-language advertisement for Gund Brewing. *Courtesy of Carl H. Miller.*

to the Great Lakes after a stint as president of a Seattle brewery. He liked his prospects in Cleveland and purchased the company in 1897.

Gund's first move was to shift the brewery's focus away, somewhat, from saloon sales. He saw potential in selling bottled beer to home consumers and added a new bottling plant in 1898. Its initial product was dubbed Gund's Crystal Bottled Beer, but the lineup grew to include Gund's Special, Gund's Finest, Ye Old Lager and Gund's Bock. The brewery was reincorporated as the Gund Brewing Company in 1900.

The Gund brewhouse and bottling plant were state-of-the-art facilities at the time. The plant boasted automatic bottle filling machines, as well as its own electric powerhouse. Gund kept ahead of packaging trends—his beer was the first in Cleveland to be distributed in cardboard cases, as opposed to traditional wooden crates, and was one of the first to feature the "Cork Crown" style of bottle cap, the direct ancestor of today's omnipresent crown cap. Gund's Finest Beer, introduced in 1912, also pioneered customer loyalty incentives. Each cardboard case held eight cartons containing three bottles, and each carton included a "Profit-Sharing" coupon that could be redeemed for merchandise from a company-published catalogue.

Upon Gund's death in 1916, his son George F. Gund II took over operations. The younger Gund introduced a new beer, Gund's Clevelander, which quickly became a local favorite. The label featured an image of Moses Cleaveland holding a mug. The slogan read, "A Wonderful City—A Wonderful Beer." The brewery's success did not last long, however, as statewide Prohibition was approved in November 1918.

Luckily for them, the Gund family had diverse investments in real estate and in other food and beverage products, including the Kaffee Hag Corporation, which pioneered decaffeinated coffee. George F. Gund II purchased Kaffee Hag for $130,000 and sold it to Kellogg's in 1927 for $10,000—mostly in Kellogg stock—a huge return on investment. Kaffee Hag is still produced today under the much more appealing and familiar name of Sanka. Gund never returned to brewing but remained the patriarch of one of the wealthiest families in Cleveland. His namesake foundation is one of the city's most recognizable charitable institutions, and his sons George Gund III and Gordon Gund owned the Cleveland Cavaliers for many years.

THE STANDARD BREWING COMPANY

Although direct sales of beer to households increased in the 1890s and early 1900s, the main retailers of beer in Cleveland remained the city's saloons. Owning a saloon was a trying business, as competition was stiff, profit margins were slim and licensing fees were high. Prohibitionist laws limited business hours and allowed residents to vote their neighborhoods dry. Worst for saloonkeepers, however, was that they often found themselves the foot soldiers in the brewers' wars against one another.

Brewers did everything they could to manipulate and control the saloon trade. They frequently bought the loyalty of saloon owners by offering lower prices than their competitors or by supplying glassware and expensive furnishings like mahogany back bars or billiard tables. Many breweries also directly owned saloons, raking in most of the profits, while providing the barest of salaries to the landlord, and if one brewery owned or controlled a saloon in a particular neighborhood, it was almost certain that a rival would establish or take control of another one nearby.

Fed up with being beholden to the beer barons, a group of Cleveland saloonkeepers banded together in 1903 to establish an alternative source of beer. The stockholders called their new venture the Standard Brewing Company and began business in a small plant on Sackett Avenue that had previously housed the Kress Weiss Beer Company. The leaders of the

A saloonkeeper strikes a pose behind the bar. *Courtesy of Carl H. Miller.*

collective were Irishmen—Stephen Creadon, who ran a saloon at West Twenty-fifth Street and Detroit Avenue, and his neighbor, John Feighan, a bank teller at the Forest City Savings Bank.

Standard's brewmaster was Jaro Pavlik, a veteran brewer, trained in his native Bohemia, who had most recently been employed at the Pilsener Brewing Company. Pavlik created Standard Old Bohemian Style Beer in honor of his homeland, but the company's famous flagship was Erin Brew—a tribute to Creadon and Feighan's Irish roots. So as not to alienate German consumers, the beer's labels also read, "Ehren Brau."

Within a year of opening, Standard relocated to the corner of Train Avenue and West Sixty-fifth Street, occupying a former flour mill. A new brewhouse, built in 1906, expanded capacity to thirty-five thousand barrels, and by 1910, production had reached seventy thousand barrels.

In 1906, the Cleveland and Sandusky Brewing Company offered to purchase Standard, but the saloon-owning stockholders refused the offer. As the company grew, however, the influence of the tavern keepers faded. By 1911, Standard had added a large number of stockholders outside of

A Standard Brewing Company delivery wagon. *Courtesy of Cleveland Public Library.*

the industry and began to focus on household beer sales. To appeal to housewives, the brewery touted the healthy, nutritious properties of its products, even describing them as "liquid food."

Like other local breweries, Standard also made a good deal of money selling ice—its Lake City Ice Company, formed in 1906, would help to carry it through Prohibition. Standard, in fact, was able to maintain a diverse business throughout Prohibition, manufacturing near beer and soft drinks and distributing dairy products, frozen food and meats. It would be the third local brewery to resume beer sales after Repeal.

THE FOREST CITY BREWING COMPANY

The third local brewery to use the Forest City moniker was established in 1904. Located on Union Avenue at East Sixty-ninth Street in the Slavic Village neighborhood, the brewery's management consisted entirely of Bohemian immigrants, including Vaclav Humel, the former president of the Pilsener Brewing Company.

The Forest City plant was an impressive five-story structure and was the first in Cleveland to feature all stainless steel brewing, fermenting and aging vessels. Its annual capacity was fifty thousand barrels. Most of its flagship product, Select Pilsner Beer, was bottled and sold to households.

At the onset of Prohibition, Forest City turned to selling de-alcoholized near beer and grape juice. It would survive Prohibition and, thanks to its modern plant, be the first Cleveland brewery to start producing beer after repeal.

THE EXCELSIOR BREWING COMPANY

Shortly after the Standard Brewing Company abandoned its first plant on Sackett Avenue, Jacob F. Haller took possession of the building and launched the Excelsior Brewing Company in 1905.

Within its first year, Excelsior produced ten thousand barrels. Soon after, the facility expanded to include a new three-story brewhouse, which increased capacity to thirty thousand barrels. The brewery marketed its

An Excelsior Brewing Company truck. *Courtesy of Carl H. Miller.*

main products, Excelsior Success Beer and Golden Seal Beer, to households. Excelsior continued to expand its facilities, even as Prohibition loomed.

It reorganized under new owner Henry Eilert as the Eilert Beverage Company in 1919 and survived most of the dry years, selling soft drinks and "near beer," although it eventually suspended operations. Eilert came out of retirement in 1933 and quickly resumed production.

THE CLEVELAND HOME BREWING COMPANY

Following his ouster from the conglomerate in March 1907, former president of the Cleveland and Sandusky Brewing Company Ernst Mueller did not waste time in getting back into the beer business. Just two months later, Mueller obtained control of the Beltz Brewing Company on the city's east side and reestablished it as the Cleveland Home Brewing Company.

The plant at East Sixty-first Street and Outhwaite Avenue was already well established at the time of Mueller's acquisition, having been in business under Joseph Beltz since 1878. Beltz started out small, brewing Weiss beer—a traditional Bavarian wheat ale, which, though popular in its

The home of Black Forest Beer, Cleveland Home Brewing Company's plant was located at 2515 East Sixty-first Street. It covered nearly an entire city block and sported a flue with "Black Forest" emblazoned on it. *Courtesy of Special Collections, Cleveland State University Archives.*

Cleveland Home Brewing Company filled some 120 barrels an hour, according to records for this pictured four-arm racker machine. Fellow workers hammered in the bungs and roll the kegs off. *Courtesy of Special Collections, Cleveland State University Archives.*

homeland and now a lucrative style for modern craft breweries, never really caught on with Cleveland's German immigrants. When his sons joined the business in 1897 and added ale and porter to its lineup, the brewery began expanding. The addition of lager beer production in 1901 increased sales to ten thousand barrels, and by the time Mueller stepped in, that figure had increased sevenfold.

Mueller quickly shifted the brewery's focus, as the new company's name suggested, from the saloon trade to sales to home consumers. Mueller knew he had neither the money nor the desire to go toe-to-toe with his former colleagues for saloon business, and he understood that home sales represented a large, still mostly untapped market.

The brewery's products—Home Beer, Meister Brau and a near beer called Yako (okay spelled backwards)—were initially packaged by an independent bottling company located next door. In 1914, the brewery opened its own bottling works.

At the onset of Prohibition, the company turned to producing ice and liquid malt. Loopholes in the Volstead Act allowed homebrewing of beer, and the company was able to keep afloat partly on sales of malt extract.

Portrait of Ernst Mueller. Mueller served as president of the Cleveland Brewing Company and on the board of the Cleveland and Sandusky combine, before opening Cleveland Home Brewing. *Courtesy of Carl H. Miller.*

Production of Yako also continued, but it never sold well. Nevertheless, the Cleveland Home Brewing Company would survive the dry years and come back a strong competitor in the city's post-Prohibition brewing scene.

Chapter 6

THE ROAD TO PROHIBITION AND OHIO'S ROLE

With its ratification certified on January 16, 1919, the National Prohibition Act came to pass in the United States on January 17, 1920, in the form of the Eighteenth Amendment to the U.S. Constitution. It was the first legislation of its kind for the country and the first to "set a time delay before it would take effect following ratification," with a full year's time expiring before the country was officially declared dry.

Modern political mythology suggests that "as Ohio goes, so goes the nation," at least as it relates to the electability of an American presidential candidate. But the roots of that statement can be traced back to the national adoption of the Eighteenth Amendment, which came on the heels of statewide prohibition that citizens approved during Ohio's November 1918 elections. The move came at the peak of four decades of fervent opposition to alcohol and was spearheaded by one of the Ohio's earliest special interest lobbyist groups: the Anti-Saloon League.

THE ANTI-SALOON LEAGUE

Formed in Oberlin in 1893, the Anti-Saloon League (ASL) took the previously held moral sentiments brewing across the country to the next level in Ohio. While the group's express purpose was conquering tavern businesses locally, such robust political traction was gained in its early work that it inevitably became a political force on a national level. It did so at a time when many politicians held more moderate or liberal political sentiments on alcohol consumption.

Standing behind the maxim "The Saloon Must Go," the ASL worked to conjoin the increasing anti-alcohol opinions of the public with political entities—first by enforcing prevailing temperance laws and then later by using those moves to further its anti-alcohol agenda through state and federal legislation.

The ASL's first informal "leader," Hiram Prince, was a multi-term Republican congressman from Iowa who—like the league's most high-profile member, the Reverend Wayne B. Wheeler—knew that the battle against alcohol wouldn't be won through individual wars against saloon owners, alcohol producers and imbibers. It would require a multitiered "moral crusade" aimed at all of them, started first with print propaganda distributed through local churches to stoke support.

While the late nineteenth century was a struggle for the organization financially, the group persevered under the formal headship of Howard Hyde Russell, a lawyer who gave up practice to become a minister. He formalized and motivated the group, reportedly raising $5 million for the temperance movement ($125 million, adjusted for current inflation) during his tenure as an anti-alcohol activist.

Russell was also the driving force behind the Lincoln-Lee Legion, an alcohol abstinence organization geared toward children and young adults, which broadened the ASL's reach into churches across the state. Awareness of the group spread like wildfire, and by 1908, there were only four states that were without similar leagues; cooperation increased from church factions all across the country.

To that end, the ASL was becoming the country's first grassroots organization to experience much broader success as a political action committee.

THE ASL: AN EARLY POLITICAL ACTION COMMITTEE

The ASL's crusade came to a frothy political head in 1905, when Wheeler launched a campaign against the reelection of incumbent Ohio governor Myron T. Herrick. A "progressive reformer," Herrick saw the inherent trouble in the increasing restriction of alcohol in the state, and when the Ohio legislature brought the 1905 Brannock Bill to the floor—which provided local communities with some autonomy over the sale of alcoholic beverages within their regions—he demanded it be ratified before he would sign it.

The revised bill stipulated that cities could only limit alcohol sales in residential neighborhoods. Herrick was still unhappy with the restriction but ultimately signed the bill. But his resistance was a bridge too far for Wheeler, who used the ASL's financial and political clout to campaign against Herrick. They initially planned to support a Republican candidate but ultimately threw their support to Democrat John M. Pattison, who defeated Herrick in his bid to return as governor.

With Herrick's ouster, other politicians in the Buckeye State became a lot more pliable (or otherwise quiet) on their views about alcohol production and consumption. After all, none of them wished to see Herrick's fate repeated in the fallout of their own political careers. Eventually, the legislature "enacted unlimited local control for communities" with the passage of the Rose Law in 1908.

At this point, brewers and distillers began to see the writing on the wall, too. Clearly, the ASL was considered a threat, described by one of its publications as a group "with unusual ability, financial capitalists with very long purses, subscribed to by hundreds of thousands of men, women and children who are solicited by their various churches, advised by well-paid attorneys of great ability."

Brewers and other "wets," as they were known, were also realizing that they weren't mobilized the way that "drys" and activist groups like the ASL were; they had only the argument of the industry bringing in as much as 20 percent of the country's tax dollars to justify their existence and figured their exemption was inevitable.

By sheer contrast, the anti-alcohol "drys" were slowly becoming something of a well-oiled political machine with sights on fundraising, lobbying and campaigning against those who disagreed with their dogmatic views. Once they saw success against alcohol interests, particularly against distilleries, they intensified their battle tenfold and took it to the front door of every brewing entity.

THE MARCH ON WASHINGTON AND THE COMING WORLD WAR

By 1913, the group's sights were trained at the federal level. ASL superintendent Purley Baker, a Methodist minister, mobilized a rally on Washington with thousands of prohibition supporters in tow. The ASL already had sympathizers seated in both houses of Congress when it arrived with its petitions and a bill that would eventually go on to inform the official Eighteenth Amendment.

Baker provided these documents to Alabama congressman Richard Hobson and Texas senator Morris Sheppard, who, in turn, introduced them to their respective legislative entities. While the early rendition of Prohibition stalled there, the ASL had, in effect, set the amendment's formal wheels in motion.

Compounding the problem for the "wets" was the war theater in Europe that eventually mutated into World War I the following year. The sinking of the RMS *Lusitania*, one of the world's largest passenger ships at the time, by a German U-boat in 1915 only helped complicate that political environment here in America—eventually pulling President Woodrow Wilson into the war.

Many of the country's brewers and distillers of the time were of German descent. With prevailing anti-German attitudes swelling in America, many German Americans were perceived as being war sympathizers at least, co-conspirators to the conflict overseas at worst.

Those negative connotations for alcohol production ("pro-beer is equivalent to pro-German") were exploited by prohibition activists, including Baker, who went on record as saying that Germans "eat like gluttons and drink like swine" and worked hard to depict anything remotely German in origin as suspect and unpatriotic.

The shortages of food in America during World War I further undermined brewers and distillers. Prohibitionists argued that the alcohol industry had a stranglehold on the nation's grain supplies, which threatened the price of food and related commodities and unpatriotically jeopardized the country's ability to feed itself during wartime.

Wheeler and the ASL found their in-road there, looking again to push the proposed Prohibition legislation. He stated, "Kaiserism abroad and booze at home must go," and threw support from ASL to President Wilson's war food control bill—suggesting that it was anti-American to use resources needed during the war effort for alcohol production.

The U.S. government agreed, putting the Food and Fuel Control Law into effect in August 1917. Also known as the "Lever Act" or the "Lever Food Act," the U.S. law prohibited the production of "distilled spirits" from any harvest that could otherwise be used as food. Grains, a critical component to beer and most distilled beverages, were suddenly off-limits.

Prohibition became a logical de facto step after that, with Ohio's statewide prohibition vote in November 1918 foreshadowing the nation's next bold move by six months' time. The political climate of wartime and the ASL's building-blocks style of activism had set the table with four previous attempts to establish statewide prohibition in Ohio during the five preceding years.

The 1917 campaign steered by ASL found over 1 million Ohio voters weighing in; it lost by a narrow margin of nearly 1,800 wet votes. The group had come a long way from its very modest beginnings, changing the course of the entire country for a thirteen-year period.

NATIONAL PROHIBITION, LOCAL BUSINESS IMPACT

National Prohibition established a total embargo on "the manufacture, sale, or transportation of intoxicating liquors within, the importation thereof

Beer being emptied into Cleveland's sewers at Leisy Brewing Company, done so under the watchful eye of Prohibition agents and federal officers (and perhaps tearful eye of Leisy brass) on October 5, 1923. *Courtesy of Special Collections, Cleveland State University Archives.*

into, or exportation thereof from the United States and all territory subject to the jurisdiction thereof for beverage purposes" by declaring beverages with more than 0.5 percent alcohol content illegal.

There were exceptions to this new law of the land—namely for religious and medical reasons—and the time gave rise to a generation of cereal beverages and near beer brews that saloon owners hoped would blunt the

Pilsener brewmaster Jaro Pavlik pours beer from a tank scheduled for de-alcoholization. *Courtesy of Special Collections, Cleveland State University Archives.*

trauma of Prohibition on business. It ushered in an era where production facilities that weren't shut down immediately were converted to produce almost-brews and more "wholesome" foodstuffs (everything from milk to juice to soft drinks) while alcohol carried on as a full-blown subculture.

Already a national force, Anheuser-Busch managed to survive Prohibition by making everything from ice cream, corn syrup and yeast to malt extract, refrigerators and automobile bodies. Here at home, the economic calamity for many breweries was just as acute, and local brewers had to adjust their business models and modernize on the fly (as Cleveland-Sandusky, Pilsener and others did) or shutter their doors (as Leisy and Diebolt did in 1923 after revising business strategies) in hopes of a repeal.

A lot of brewers simply weren't prepared for a shift in business; the ones that did implemented the use of "de-alcoholizing" machines, which reduced the alcohol content in the brewing process to create near beer products.

Cleveland and Sandusky Brewing Company was particularly active in producing alternative beverages during Prohibition, all in the hopes that saloon business could survive without serving alcohol. It produced several near beers for distribution in Ohio, including the "Gold Bond Beverage" called Bola—which was marketed as "healthful, nutritious and invigorating," as well as "cool, sparkling and foamy." It also produced Starlight, New York Special Brew and Crystal Rock, as well as a number of soft drinks, including Johnny Bull Ginger Beer, Brownie Chocolate and an orange-flavored pick-me-up called Whistle Orange.

In a move that mirrored the silence from political officials after Governor Herrick's ouster before Prohibition, Cleveland and Sandusky (and other breweries) rebranded themselves—presumably in an attempt to put distance between them from the stigma associated with beer production. The new Cleveland-Sandusky Company name showcased this new business model, just as it hoped to avoid damage to its public perception in the process.

Pilsener Brewing Company and Diebolt Brewing Company made similar overtures to the public with new names and faces in the marketplace. Both produced a host of "special brew" items and soft drinks. The former had modest success with "Parfay" (a cola-style beverage that was produced in various iterations by other regional brewers) and ginger ale; the latter struggled with the "wholesome and refreshing" Perlex malt beverage. They also renamed themselves in the same way Cleveland-Sandusky did. The former became the Pilsener Ice, Fuel and Beverage Company in 1928, with subsequent advertising referring to it as "P.O.C. Products Co."

While Pilsener survived Prohibition, Diebolt wasn't as fortunate—ceasing all beverage production in 1923 after refreshing its moniker as the Diebolt Company and also selling ice under its parallel business arm, the Cleveland Hygeia Ice Company. Ice was a popular side business for many breweries, including Standard and Cleveland Home Brewing Company, which already had infrastructure in place to produce it for local distributors in a wholesale business model.

Leisy, which had also produced a near beer called Bevera since 1917, also shuttered in 1923 after diversifying its beverage portfolio with items like "Old Fashion Root Beer." What's more, its "The Isaac Leisy Co." labeling also attempted to put some distance between it and its beer-related past. But that wasn't enough to overcome poor sales. Rebranding proved that a brewery's struggle to remain economically viable in this new dry world was real.

Of all the Cleveland-based breweries, Leisy and Cleveland-Sandusky had the most varied range of bottled beverages to offer the public—including root beer, orangeade, ginger ale and loganberry-flavored soft drinks, and near beer beverages. But all of that business diversification didn't necessarily equate to survival.

While cereal beverages, soft drinks, dairy products and juices opened brewers to new retail outlets (drug- and grocery stores among them), cereal beverages never caught on in saloons, never experienced popularity levels that producers hoped for in the long run and simply couldn't compete with the illegal beer and related alcohol underground taking root across the region and the country.

Other Prohibition-Era Business Diversification for Brewers

Not all brewers stuck with foodstuffs and beverages as a means of branching out. By proxy, some brewers became real estate magnates, having invested heavily in large-scale properties for production and small-scale storefront saloons, which they had purchased prior to prohibition. These brewers had become experts in how to value, manage and transfer real estate and generally navigate the property business.

The Diebolt brothers, who had already shut down their brewery in 1923 due to poor sales, were among the more active Cleveland entities in such endeavors. Sadly, their biggest real estate transaction didn't fall their way.

The Diebolt's brewery and ice plant located on Pittsburgh Avenue fell into a bitter eminent domain court battle with Oris and Mantis Van Sweringen, the developers who built Cleveland's Union Terminal (now Terminal Tower). The case raged over five years, with the Van Sweringens winning the right to raze the property for railroad traffic right-of-way into the terminal. The brewery was razed in 1928.

In stark contrast, the Gund family amassed wealth and retained great presence in Cleveland as a result of their brewery-related real estate (and other) dealings. Outside of selling former saloon properties, they made a couple of extremely savvy business moves, wisely anticipating the future business landscape for brewers.

When Ohio's statewide prohibition was adopted, George F. Gund II sold off his inventory of beer to Pilsener Brewing Company and purchased the Kaffee Hag (German for "coffee grove") Corporation. He sequestered this new business in the old brewery, and marketed the decaf java as "Night Cap Coffee," before reverting back to the original name. Within two years, he had made the aforementioned deal with the Kellogg Company for $10 million. Eventually, that decaf became Sanka.

Needless to say, the Gund name is still one synonymous with Cleveland, in diverse entrepreneurial areas ranging from philanthropy to professional sports.

ALCOHOL, ORGANIZED CRIME AND SPEAKING EASY

While legitimized production and distribution of alcohol had halted across the country, organized crime picked up the dropped baton and ran with it. Prohibition became an era of bootleggers, who would produce their own alcohol for clandestine sale and consumption; of rumrunners, who illegally trafficked these products across state lines for resale; of cocktail parties, where said bootleggers' wares found their way to a buyer's family, neighbors and friends in secret celebrations; and to illegal speakeasies (also known as "blind pigs" or "blind tigers"), which quietly served those not buying into the high-moral notion of America's "Noble Experiment."

Prohibition became an era of rampant gangster activity—with criminal gangs going to war with one another over the control of a region's underground alcohol business. In 1919, a year before Prohibition was enacted, Cleveland was said to have some 1,000–1,200 legitimate bars conducting legal business.

But by 1923, the city had an estimated 2,500–3,000 illegal speakeasies, "along with 10,000 stills." Estimates also suggest that as many as 30,000 Cleveland residents "sold liquor during Prohibition, and another 100,000 made home brew or bathtub gin for themselves and friends."

Underground speakeasies became very popular among those who wished to continue alcohol consumption. Nearly all had private memberships so as to avoid the prying eyes of temperance officials and local law enforcement.

The Cleveland area had many notable speakeasies, including the Blaue Club (located in the 4100 block of St. Clair Avenue), Sinclair Avenue Place, the Hamilton Street Central Athletic Club, the pub now known as Stone Mad in the Gordon Square Arts District, the Beacon House (which later became Fagan's in the Flats) and the Sachsenheim Club—not to be confused with the historic German beer hall on Dennison Avenue—which was located at 1400 East Fifty-fifth Street.

Raids against speakeasies were fraught with difficulty, in large part because law enforcement officials weren't particularly effective in busting potentially illegal activity happening in them. Proof of wrongdoing seemed difficult to pin down at many locations; near beer was often on hand to throw off the scent.

What's more, both local authorities and the federal law enforcement agency Bureau of Prohibition weren't beyond corruption themselves. Agents weren't above taking a bribe to turn a blind eye away from (and point an empty glass toward) the activity happening.

The level of lawlessness was especially striking, given that the Association Against the Prohibition Amendment (AAPA) formed almost immediately following the Eighteenth Amendment's ratification. Corporate entities and American labor organizations quickly lined up in support of the AAPA, suggesting that lower business tax revenues would be passed on to individuals in the form of higher taxes. AAPA leaders also intimated it would also lead to a higher rate of crime.

They couldn't have been more right. During Cleveland's "dry years," it was estimated that over one hundred "violent deaths" could be attributed to clandestine booze business. Just as shocking was the local scandal surrounding the Million Dollar Hair Tonic Company, said to have trafficked upward of $1 million in pure grain alcohol through barbershops disguised as "Love Me Dearie" hair tonic. Two Cleveland barbers fell within law enforcement crosshairs as a part of the city's crackdown.

Organized crime related to alcohol took hold in a number of pockets throughout Cleveland, with Little Italy's Mayfield Road Mob being one of the more infamous groups. Fronted by the Porello brothers, the mob was feared and revered in the same way Al Capone was in Chicago—their claim to fame being the import of bootleg beer and liquor from Canada.

As a result of Prohibition, organized crime became de rigueur in the city—so much so that whole books are devoted to organized crime in Cleveland and the activity here. It was even worthy enough to merit a mention in the 1972 Academy Award-winning film *The Godfather*, in which certain mob factions were alluded to with a veiled "Lakeview Road Gang" reference, a nod to the proximity of Lakeview Cemetery to Mayfield Road Hill.

Local law enforcement struggled to combat this illicit activity on multiple fronts. Already woefully underfunded and understaffed, police had their victories against "demon drinks" here and there, but they were largely obscured by a subculture of secretive excess. Success at shutting down these diverse alcohol outlets required complex infiltration into the illegal operations, a hearty slate of constabulary informants and the immeasurable patience required to ferret out leads.

In the end, pro-alcohol groups and organizations realized that the only way to fight fire was with said fire. Taking a page from the ASL playbook, the Moderation League, the Crusaders, the Women's Organization for National Prohibition Reform and other anti-prohibitionists made an impact through their own political action committee activities.

They also found sympathizers in Clevelander Robert J. Bulkley (of Bulkley Building Company fame), who was elected to the U.S. Senate in 1930 on a repeal platform, and in then-presidential candidate Franklin D. Roosevelt, who was very much pro-repeal when measured against his "Noble Experiment"–coining opponent, Republican Herbert Hoover.

Rounding out the perfect storm against Prohibition was the onset of the Great Depression. The economic disaster lent credence to the notions that a) the United States may have plunged into financial tumult in part because of tax revenue lost by forbidding alcohol sales and b) that the federal government should not be attempting to "police morality" during such a financially difficult time.

Cleveland, which had been a booming city during the Roaring Twenties, struggled mightily during Prohibition and with it the blue-collar factions who had kept the city ticking until the job market dried up with the Depression. To that faction in particular, Roosevelt's inauguration would whet the palate in more ways than one, with work and after-work beverages making for a particularly sweet reward.

Chapter 7
REFORM, REPEAL AND REBIRTH

Cleveland's Beer Business Returns

Even before president-elect Roosevelt took office, there were signs that Prohibition would eventually fall. Unemployment was rising, and the GDP was falling all over the world, not just in the United States. Across the country, unemployment had reached an average of 25 percent. Cities like Cleveland, with huge blue-collar populations and workforces of laborers with heavy industry experience, were hit even harder by the Great Depression.

The situation forced Washington to reexamine the moral experiment with a much needed reality check. Congress had already given itself the right, in the Volstead Act, to determine what qualified as an "intoxicating beverage." It eventually approved the Cullen Bill, a piece of legislation that made legal the sale of 3.2 percent alcohol-by-weight beer. It was passed on April 7, 1933.

While this move didn't formally end or repeal Prohibition, it certainly took the teeth out of its bite. The bill generated tax revenue to the tune of $5 of federal tax per barrel and a $1,000 annual licensing fee for each brewery opening or reopening in its wake. It also undermined the rampant crime that had resulted from illegal alcohol and put people back to work—starting with everyone in and related to the brewing business. Prohibition was repealed, not much later, with the passing of the Twenty-first Amendment.

Across the country, revelry ensued with the Cullen Bill's ratification; here at home, lawyer turned Ohio state senator Joseph Ackerman of Shaker Heights represented the state's beer interests with the passing of the Ackerman Bill a week before, a document that ostensibly mirrored the Cullen Bill's mission. He returned home by train, arriving at Union Terminal to a hero's welcome:

thousands had flooded Public Square. Like a modern-day athlete who had won the big game, he was hoisted upon Cleveland's shoulders and carried off to a celebration.

It should be noted that the public celebration was officially "dry" in accordance with then-mayor Raymond T. Miller's decree that no beer would be sold before April 7.

ROLL OUT THE BARREL

While Cleveland's drinkers celebrated this springtime "New Beer's Day," the region's brewers were unprepared to have their products ready for consumption. Beer arrived from outside the city for the big day, while a coalition of Cleveland's main brewers—Standard, Pilsener, Eilert, Forest City, Cleveland-Sandusky and Cleveland Home Brewing Company—alerted the public that it didn't want to release an "inferior product" that wasn't properly aged and that its wares would soon be available again for public consumption.

These brewers knew it wouldn't be long. After all, those who had been making near beer throughout the Prohibition era had little trouble getting geared back up to produce their fans' foamy favorites.

By stark contrast, Leisy (and perhaps to a larger extent, Cleveland-Sandusky) had a tougher row to hoe. While the old Leisy brewery had been shuttered, it didn't exactly fold like other breweries did. The family was still intent on brewing beer, and the facilities were still available. But given that their equipment was auctioned off during the furlough, there was a need for quick retooling and re-equipping to start up again.

Cleveland-Sandusky was in an even tougher spot but managed to fare better than Leisy, at least initially. Not only did it have some revamping to do, but it was so financially strapped for cash that head brewer Hascal C. Lang desperately approached his investors and stockholders with the notion that without some liquid assets, there would be no "liquid assets" to sell. It would take until mid-summer of 1933 for its beverages to arrive, but once they did, the Crystal Rock and Gold Bond brands were among Cleveland's more popular choices.

Pilsener was the first to return to the marketplace, releasing its first batch of P.O.C. beer for public consumption in early May 1933. At that point, it, like many other brewers across the nation, halted all substitute/

Left: Men greet the first shipments of beer to Cleveland, post-Prohibition, in 1933. *Courtesy of Cleveland Public Library.*

Below: Beer from Chicago arrives in Cleveland at the end of Prohibition. Cleveland's resumed production was a little slow to start; outside brews helped fend off the lag time and fulfill the immediate demand for beer. *Courtesy of Cleveland Public Library.*

A worker at Pilsener Brewing Company stacks beer barrels for refilling. *Courtesy of Cleveland Public Library.*

alternate beverage production that had formerly kept its business afloat to accommodate beer demands. By the mid-1930s, it was producing 175,000 barrels, an estimate that suggested a modest increase in production prior to Prohibition.

Cleveland Home Brewing Company's was next to market. Its "Clevelander" beer brand arrived at the end of that month, resurrecting the name that the Gunds had utilized for one of their signature brews. This was followed with a number of other varieties of beer, including Meister Brau. Next came Standard, which returned its popular Erin Brew on the market at the end of May as well. Standard, like many other Cleveland brewers, struggled to keep up with demand.

Eilert, which had anticipated a potential repeal of Prohibition, planned to have its products available the moment restrictions were lifted. What the brewer hadn't anticipated was a complex lawsuit brought by former shareholders of the Eilert Beverage Company or its inability to issue new stock.

Although Leisy kicked into overdrive with renovations, its product wouldn't return to market until the following summer. Fortunately for the company, Cleveland beer drinkers had a long memory, and that boded well for its production. Plant capacity stood at 120,000 barrels when it reopened, and by the end of that same summer, it had doubled. Leisy's Premium and Special Brew products were among the top sellers and helped to return the brand (and family) to the number one spot in its renewed ad campaigns, as well as Cleveland's beer sales charts.

REGULATION, TAXATION AND NEW COMPETITION

As in many major cities, Cleveland experienced a beer renaissance, but it was not without bumps. After all, the Depression was still on, and while production was in high gear, at least initially, brewers were mired in a whole host of new government regulations. They also faced a swift drop-off in sales, new state and federal taxes and a price war that threatened to unsettle the Cleveland Brewers Association, which had been ostensibly established to keep prices stable. A brief but feisty price war ensued.

Cleveland's brewers were also the center of controversy in April 1935, when disputes between brewery workers and teamsters forced a

Brewery workers on strike. *Courtesy of Special Collections, Cleveland State University Archives.*

strike that dragged on until the end of the year. Violence, abrupt clashes and blockades dotted the brewing landscape. As a result of the unrest, Cleveland-Sandusky was forced to close its Stang plant in Sandusky and move production east to Cleveland.

Adding to all of the drama was new local competition in the form of Sunrise Brewing Company.

SUNRISE BREWING COMPANY

Sunrise arose from the remnants of the Gund Brewing Company, which itself was a very successful brewing entity throughout its lifespan—remaining in operation until statewide Prohibition took effect in 1919. The Gund lakefront plant, still owned by the Gund Realty Company as a part of its business diversification, had been vacant for many years (also serving as a small malt syrup purveyor in the late 1920s) and required an intense amount of modernization. Repeal brought a reestablishment of the brewery; it was officially resurrected and newly christened as the Sunrise Brewing Company in 1933.

The Sunrise Brewery Building, which was located on Davenport Avenue. *Courtesy of Cleveland Public Library.*

For a time, Tip Top and other brewers across the country were using a tear-off bottle cap. This 1940 photo features its Bohemian beer bottle with this aluminum cap technology. *Courtesy of Special Collections, Cleveland State University Archives.*

During its nearly six-year tenure, Sunrise produced an eponymous beer, the brightly named Golden Dawn, and a number of other old-style ales with German roots. The mechanical overhaul left the brewing company sitting pretty when demand peaked; the plant's annual capacity reached upward of seventy-five thousand barrels initially, and nearly doubled with additional improvements.

But Sunrise's lifespan was not without hullabaloo: nearly a year into its business, the brewery faced a slew of federal charges that ranged from fraud of recycling the tax-stamps of kegs to falsified production output documents.

Resulting fines forced the resignation of top officials (former Standard executive and Sunrise vice-president Jaro Pavlik remained as brewmaster) and the ultimate sale of the business to Harry and David Frankel.

Pavlik introduced a pair of new beers to the public during his thirty-fifth year as a brewmaster: Cheerio Ale and Tip-Top Beer. Eventually, rampant sales of Tip-Top Beer resulted in a name change. The site itself remained in business, post-branding change, as the Tip-Top Brewing Company. It remained until 1944—when wartime rations, liquor violations and Chicago mob ties unraveled the business.

A Whole New World

After Prohibition, the beer business had shifted in a number of ways—namely in terms of greater automation, motorized trucking for delivery and even in the vehicle by which consumers themselves actually consumed the beer.

Women demonstrate how the new bottling machinery works at Cleveland and Sandusky. *Courtesy of Special Collections, Cleveland State University Archives.*

A view of the Standard Brewing Company complex, looking eastward down Train Avenue. Most of the buildings remain today. *Courtesy of Special Collections, Cleveland State University Archives.*

Draft/draught beer was no longer the preferred means of consumption. Packaged beer in bottles and later in metal cans won favor with larger "shipping" brewers. This preference paved the early steps to consolidation in the marketplace: smaller brewers were able to maintain their cult audiences without expending capital, while larger brewers with bigger pocketbooks utilized their resources to advertise and proliferate, taking up market share from those who couldn't afford to keep up with further modernization, ad campaigns and the like.

By all accounts, Cleveland had nine different breweries operating in 1939, which employed nearly 1,300 people and produced upward of $10 million in alcoholic beverage sales annually. And while many of those entities implemented new strategies to continue their growth—Standard Brewing Company among them, with a hefty plant expansion that cost millions of dollars and expanded the territory into adjoining states—emerging national brands were poised to take a bite out of Cleveland.

CARLING BREWING COMPANY

Peerless automobile manufacturer James A. Bohannon came to his shareholders with a bold statement in the summer of 1931: given the current economic climate, he said, automobile production was a losing proposition and he had decided to revert their plant in Cleveland to a brewery.

Enter the Brewing Corporation of America on Quincy Avenue. It was a far cry from the luxury cars the company was used to producing, but Bohannon did not see the company (as it existed) surviving the Depression.

Not all of Peerless's executives jumped at the idea at first, despite the signs that Prohibition's day were numbered. But they were rewarded

Portrait of Carling president James A. Bohannon. *Courtesy of Special Collections, Cleveland State University Archives.*

once the Peerless plant was converted (under the watchful eye of one J.C. Schultz) and reopened as a brewery in 1934.

Being an automobile guy (an industry that is anything but local), Bohannon didn't feel the need to limit business to his locality. That was his reasoning for bringing in Canadian brewer Carling—née Carling O'Keefe, a recognized brand of Canadian Breweries, Ltd., and its subsequent know-how to increase production.

It didn't open up new vistas quite as planned, at least initially. Bohannon had licensed Carling's processes with the idea that its Red Cap ale, a lighter beer brewed in Canada since 1840, would be a huge draw locally—namely with drinkers recalling bootlegged beer arriving from across Lake Erie.

As it happened, Carling's "Black Label," a more budget-friendly brew, would be Bohannon's saving grace. Black Label was right for the time: an economically viable brand for Cleveland, given that all of America was still in financial dire straits. The modest beer appealed to a cash-strapped audience, pushing Carling's (and Bohannon's) profits decidedly upward.

Left: Carling Brewing Company Building. The former automobile plant at East Ninety-third Street and Quincy Avenue is now the site of Cuyahoga County's Juvenile Justice Center. *Courtesy of Cleveland Public Library.*

Below: A trio of Carling Black Label promotional puppets, a part of a "retail display" that became more active in the commercial marketing era for beer. Collectors of breweriana often seek out these and other vintage advertising items. *Courtesy of Special Collections, Cleveland State University Archives.*

Like many other large breweries sprouting up across the country, Carling used "aggressive merchandising" to cement its industry standing. As its star continued to rise, Carling sales cracked the top twenty in the nation, became a multi-plant operation and, perhaps inevitably, became Cleveland's largest brewing entity.

By 1944, Carling had reached fifteenth in national sales and was suddenly in a position to snatch up smaller competing breweries. Cleveland's Tip-Top and Forest City breweries were casualties of their aggressive buying strategy.

His outsider's strategy (both in the industry and in using a more corporate-style approach to marketing) didn't endear Bohannon or Carling to other local brewers who were trying to keep a toehold with their audience.

It hardly mattered. That same year, Bohannon sold his stock holdings to Canadian Breweries, Ltd., giving that firm controlling interest in his business. Carling carried on for a while as an impressive brewer with a strong American foundation in the Cleveland market. But that, like so many things in the brewing landscape, was about to change…

Chapter 8

RENAISSANCE, CONSOLIDATION AND DECLINE IN THE ADVERTISING AGE

The repeal of Prohibition was a double-edged sword for the local beer industry. On one hand, the ensuing beer boom and surging production ensured that imbibers would have plenty of volume and options to choose from. Nationally, per capita beer consumption between 1939 and 1945 experienced a 52 percent increase—climbing from 12.3 to 18.7 gallons.

Once federal restrictions on grain were lifted two years later, that boom grew even bigger, even if it only lasted a short time. But with that boom came increased competition from inside and outside the city, all of it fierce: price wars, and a hearty, amplified advertising blitz from brewers, all in an effort to corner a greater market share.

Brewers also had to adapt to the fact that beer consumption and American life itself had changed. Corner taverns were no longer the only game in town when it came to consumption; packaged beverages and the rise in electric refrigerators gradually replacing the icebox saw to that.

All of the major players in Cleveland's brewing landscape executed some sort of upgrade, plant expansion or process improvement plan—all to ensure they could keep up with the demand. Beer was suddenly a lot more desirable in bottles or flat-top or cone-top cans, and making these vessels disposable added plenty of convenience and mobility.

Leisy was an early adopter of this new beer technology, and its Leisy Schooner (a "throwaway bottle... with can-like shape") ushered in a new era of brewing business in which an imbiber's location wasn't prohibitive to consumption.

Right: A worker at Pilsener inspects enormous fermenting tanks in the beer cellar. *Courtesy of Cleveland Public Library.*

Below: "The temperature of Carling's ale produced at the former Peerless automobile plant at Cleveland is controlled at every step of the process…" in this 1945 Cleveland Press photo. Beer was often examined in front of lightboxes for quality control. *Courtesy of Special Collections, Cleveland State University Archives.*

Pilsener's P.O.C. cans getting filled. *Courtesy of Carl H. Miller.*

So revolutionary was the approach that in 1945, Brewing Corporation's president Bohannon (somewhat rashly) decided to forgo draught beer and bottles with deposits and move to discard-only beer vessels to appeal to a larger audience. The move proved costly, as consumers were still in wartime mindsets and saw disposable items as wasteful. The company eventually reverted back to paid-deposit glass bottles.

As Goes Leisy, So Goes the Industry

Leisy was among the most successful of the brewers during this time period, attributing the aforementioned doubling of production to a major rebuild with all new equipment in 1934. Among its augmentations was a "modern bottling complex" on Vega Avenue, though it was also fairly aggressive in implementing an updated fleet of delivery vehicles, steel beer can technology (although Standard claimed to be first to the market

Above: The Leisy Brewing Company delivery fleet stands ready to route Cleveland-produced beer to the surrounding city and suburbs. *Courtesy of Cleveland Public Library.*

Right: Brewing a batch of Leisy's beer. *Courtesy of Carl H. Miller.*

with such technology in the area) and four-gallon growlers—large party keg–style vessels that required a hand-pump to dispense the beer within.

As a result of modernization, Leisy was among the steadiest of local brewers post-repeal and remained one of the city's top three beer sales leaders until the mid-1950s. At its peak, Leisy produced some 330,000 barrels annually but ultimately lost the top sales spot in 1948 to Standard Brewing Company.

But industrial modernization was only a part of this post-Prohibition world. The transformation of mass media and advertising at the time was increasingly chaotic—American brewers were spending $95 million on advertising annually by the 1960s, compared only to $6 million in the late 1930s. Adjusted for inflation, this represented a more than 1,300 percent increase in expenditures that had not previously been required (just as disposable bottling costs were).

Brewers here and elsewhere couldn't put that toothpaste back in the tube. It was a brave new world for brewers, and a whole new level of competition was on.

Sell! Sell! Sell!

Ah, advertising. It's so ubiquitous in the twenty-first century that it can often be taken for granted or simply tuned out. But during this brewing renaissance in Cleveland, marketing and promotion was becoming every bit as important to a brewery's livelihood as the ingredients in the product itself. Leisy made sure its advertising was everywhere, from busses to billboards to bars.

But so did much of its competition, and in all manner of venues, too, including the tried-and-true avenues of print and radio advertising, as well as in a surging new technology: television. TV caused everyone to step his proverbial ad game up—both literally and figuratively.

Standard, which, along with Cleveland Home Brewing, had been a fairly steady brand for the area, found new success in televised advertising. It hired revered Indians play-by-play broadcaster Jimmy Dudley as its pitchman and successfully implemented an ad campaign for Erin Brew tied to the red-hot Cleveland Indians, who won the World Series that year. Standard would remain in the top sales spot until 1951, with increased visibility throughout the majority of what Cleveland beer historian Carl H. Miller dubbed the "Fatal Fifties" of brewery decline.

UNDERGROUND RATHSKELLER WHERE LEISY'S WAS LAGERED IN OLDEN DAYS

ACTUALLY AGED LONGER — LEISY'S IS CLEVELAND'S FAVORITE BREW — SINCE 1862

A postcard illustrating Leisy Brewing Company's rathskeller. After the introduction of artificial refrigeration, the brewery converted its obsolete lagering tunnels into an underground party facility. *Courtesy of Carl H. Miller.*

A tin tray advertising Standard Brewing Company's flagship Erin Brew. Erin Brew signage and packaging featured the phrase "Ehren Brau" to avoid alienating German consumers. *Courtesy of Carl H. Miller.*

A Gold Bond beer tin sign. Gold Bond was the Fishel Brewing Company's flagship and became one of the Cleveland and Sandusky Brewing Company's best-selling offerings after Fishel was absorbed into the combine. *Courtesy of Carl H. Miller.*

An L. Schlather Brewing Company tin tray. The Schlather Brewery was one of the largest brewing concerns in Cleveland prior to Prohibition. *Courtesy of Carl H. Miller.*

A Sunrise Brewing Company beer tray. Sunrise Brewing Company evolved, after Prohibition, from the defunct Gund Brewing Company. *Courtesy of Carl H. Miller.*

Tap handles and chalkboard at the Bottlehouse in Cleveland Heights. The handmade metal handles are typical of the brewery's freewheeling, do-it-yourself aesthetic. *Photo by Leslie Basalla.*

Above: An interior view of the Taphouse at Fat Heads. The Taphouse, which opened in 2013, is housed in Fat Heads' Middleburg Heights production brewery. *Photo by Leslie Basalla.*

Left: Nano Brew Cleveland on West Twenty-fifth Street is the sister brewery to Market Garden and features a bicycle theme. *Photo by Leslie Basalla.*

Platform Beer Company on the western edge of Ohio City is Ohio's first brewery incubator. Its building once housed a Hungarian social club that featured the city's first ten-pin bowling alleys. *Photo by Leslie Basalla.*

A plastic sign advertising Pilsener Brewing Company's P.O.C. Beer. This is sign is part of an extensive collection of vintage breweriana on display at the Brew Kettle in Strongsville. *Photo by Leslie Basalla.*

Bar patrons at Platform Brewing Company's grand opening. Platform's elegant draft system comes courtesy of co-owner Justin Carson's other business, JC Beertech. *Courtesy of Shaun Yasaki/Platform Beer Co.*

A panoramic shot of the fermenters at Butcher and the Brewer. The brewery's cellar area is open to public viewing and occasionally plays host to private dinners and events. *Courtesy of Mike Gorek.*

Assorted vintage bottles and a Standard Brewing Company sign adorn a window at Prosperity Social Club in Cleveland's Tremont neighborhood. *Courtesy of Bonnie Flinner/ Prosperity Social Club.*

Portside Distillery and Brewery's tap handles are handmade in the likeness of the lighthouse that sits at the entrance to Cleveland's harbor. *Photo by Leslie Basalla.*

Great Lakes Brewing Company's many flagship and seasonal offerings on display in a beer cooler in the brewery's gift shop. *Photo by Leslie Basalla.*

Great Lakes Brewing Company founders Pat and Dan Conway share a toast in the brewery's taproom in this photo taken on the company's twenty-fifth anniversary in 2013. *Courtesy of Great Lakes Brewing Co.*

Above: The brewhouse at Great Lakes Brewing Company is the largest and most high-tech in the city. *Courtesy of Great Lakes Brewing Co.*

Right: Willoughby Brewing Company brewmaster Rick Seibt poses behind the bar of the historic brewpub. *Courtesy of Willoughby Brewing Co.*

Left: Willoughby Brewing Company's bar and brewhouse. Opened in 1998, Willoughby is one of the area's longest-running and most successful breweries. *Courtesy of Willoughby Brewing Co.*

Below: A couple enjoys a round in the beer garden at Market Garden Brewery. Market Garden is one of several breweries located in the burgeoning Ohio City neighborhood. *Photo by Lindsey Beckwith.*

Beer flights at Platform are served in caddies made of wood reclaimed from the bowling alley floor inside the building. *Photo by Leslie Basalla.*

Bottles wait to be filled on Fat Heads bottling line. The production brewery is slowly expanding to package seasonal beers as well as flagships Head Hunter and Bumbleberry. *Photo by Leslie Basalla.*

Members of the brewing staff at Fat Heads conduct a taste-testing panel. This quality control measure is a weekly ritual for the brewers. *Photo by Leslie Basalla.*

Fat Heads pub brewer Mike Zoscak stirs a kettle in the North Olmsted brewpub's brewhouse. *Photo by Leslie Basalla.*

Right: Platform Beer Company brewmaster Shaun Yasaki tests wort from a batch of beer to determine if it has reached the correct sugar content, or original gravity. *Photo by Leslie Basalla.*

Below: Platform Beer Company assistant brewer Reed Jasulka gets his beard steamed as he stirs a batch of grain in the brewery's mash tun. *Photo by Leslie Basalla.*

Left: Fat Heads' flagship beer, Head Hunter, a West Coast–style IPA, has won many awards, as this wall mural at the brewery attests. *Photo by Leslie Basalla.*

Below: Bartender Tom Owen fills a flight of four beer samples at Market Garden Brewery. *Photo by Leslie Basalla.*

Right: Patrons enjoy a visit to Buckeye Brewing Company's tasting room, Tapstack. The bottle chandelier and blue sky–themed walls are reflective of brewer/owner Garin Wright's fun and funky aesthetic. *Photo by Leslie Basalla.*

Below: Nano Brew Cleveland underwent an expansion in 2015 that included a major renovation of its patio and outdoor bar. The beer garden is one of the most popular drinking destinations in the Ohio City neighborhood. *Photo by Leslie Basalla.*

A close-up view of a beer flight at Market Garden Brewery. The brewery usually has between ten and fourteen house beers on draft, and samplers allow guests to taste several varieties in small quantities. *Photo by Leslie Basalla.*

Chalkboard signs at Brick and Barrel advertise its growlers, displayed here. *Photo by Leslie Basalla.*

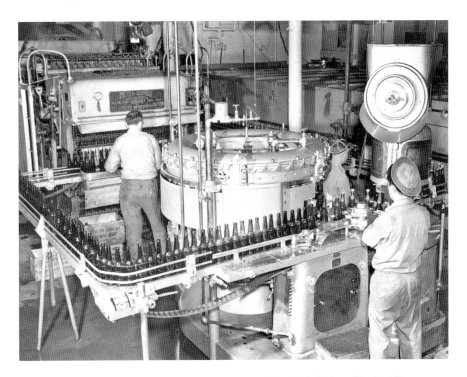

Cleveland-Sandusky's bottling apparatus. *Courtesy of Special Collections, Cleveland State University Archives.*

Standard wasn't the only brewer to court the Indians. Leisy did likewise, stepping up with a large sponsorship package ($75,000) for the Indians in 1949 to televise alternating home games. Indians pitcher Tris Speaker and local color commentator Bob Neal were hired by Leisy to call the games. At one point, a Leisy's World Series Beer honoring the Indians was also considered for release, but that idea was shelved in lieu of other more immediate marketing campaign ideas.

Like Leisy, Cleveland-Sandusky (previously Cleveland and Sandusky before Prohibition) had effectively modernized its plants to distribute its beers to a far larger delivery radius. Cleveland-Sandusky followed in Leisy's footsteps in production, too, increasing to 200,000 barrels of output from 120,000 in a relatively short time.

Its also ran some effective marketing strategies from its own "playbook." C-S implemented a campaign tied to the sports championships of another Cleveland team: the NFL's Cleveland Browns. Then C-S president Homer Marshman—who himself had ties to the previous Cleveland Rams football team in the 1930s—implemented a strategy surrounding the Browns'

P.O.C.'s Golden Girl, the sultrier answer to Carling's "Black Label" Mabel. *Courtesy of Carl H. Miller.*

A Pilsener Brewing Company "P.O.C." billboard, emphasizing one of its slogans, "Pilsener P.O.C. since 1893—our hand has never lost its skill." *Courtesy of Special Collections, Cleveland State University Archives.*

championship franchise and, by the mid-1950s, was sponsoring Browns television broadcasts. C-S brands Old Timers Ale and Gold Bond Beer were cornerstones of the campaign.

Pilsener fell in line with this new "advertising age" for beer in Cleveland, too—and did so quite effectively. It sponsored televised boxing matches and the American Hockey League's Cleveland Barons hockey games, lent its name to the *All Outdoors* and *P.O.C. Saturday Night Sports Club* television programs and even recruited Cleveland native, comedian and consummate vaudevillian Bob Hope to be the face of its campaigns. Brewery president George Carter was a childhood friend of Hope's; both had shared childhood dreams of being professional boxers.

Clearly, even from the late 1940, brewers saw professional sports as a means to hawk their wares through advertising; televisions were becoming de rigueur in taverns across the country. Professional sports were becoming king, and what better way to direct-market beer than to the folks parked on barstools watching the games?

Solely dedicated "sports bars" would come along many years later, but surely the genesis of them began in this newly minted advertising age where beer and "ball" walked hand in hand.

THE FOREST FOR THE TREES

As history sadly recounts, no one survived this post-Prohibition "commercial" era for beer in Cleveland, but some brands were quicker to bow out than others—often times with a less-prolific advertising strategy at least partially to blame for their curtain call. Because competition had stiffened throughout the country, particularly from national brands against the home team brewers, advertising and price cuts continued to wear away at profits.

Making matters worse, shades of the previous world war repeated themselves during World War II in the rationing of hops and malt under the War Food Order 66. The restrictions severely hampered brewery production. Following the war, however, brewers experienced another boom. With this and all the other post-Prohibition upheaval, brewers in Cleveland and across the country never really were allowed leveled-out sales or a predictable production trajectory.

Cleveland-Sandusky president (and brewmaster of the time) Frank P. van de Westelaken was one of the first to see this danger when he reported

A look at a modern can-sealing of the time at the Standard Brewing Company. A Standard worker loads can-tops into the machine, while cans of Erin Brew move down the conveyor belt to be sealed. *Courtesy of Special Collections, Cleveland State University Archives.*

A bar receives a delivery of Cleveland Home Brewing's flagship Meister Brau. *Courtesy of Carl H. Miller.*

positive growth for his company in 1946, but warned of a perfect storm of "higher cost of materials, and much more pronounced competition," adding that both would combine to make it "increasingly difficult to maintain a respectable profit margin between the selling price of our product and the cost to produce it."

Two years later, in 1948, all of the government rationing was over, and Standard was perhaps the most poised to take advantage: its ongoing bottling-and-canning plant expansion (replete with $4.5 million price tag) was completed in 1950 and upped the brewer's annual output from 400,000 to 550,000 barrels. The company used its revolutionary new operation to expand Erin Brew distribution to parts of New York, Pennsylvania and Michigan.

Cleveland Home, on the other hand, was hit by this era especially hard. Already reeling from the deaths of president Omar Mueller (son of Prohibition-era president Ernst Mueller) and brewmaster George Lezius, the brewery continued to experience decreases in production during the late 1940s. After peaking with an output of 175,000 barrels during its heyday, the revered Black Forest Beer brewer's manufacture fell off by nearly 80 percent and, by 1952, had run aground financially and was shuttered for good—but not before making several attempts to diversify its premium beer stable. It was the first postwar casualty in Cleveland brewers' ongoing battle for beer market share.

Lagging Leisy Languishes

Cleveland Home was far from the only one to experience trouble. Even the local heavy-hitters weren't exempt. The year 1952 marked the ninetieth anniversary of the Leisy family's brewing tradition. They released an anniversary beer to commemorate it, along with hosting a celebration for their 300 millionth gallon of brew produced. Sales, however, weren't commensurate with such festivity. In fact, like those of its contemporaries, Leisy's sales were on a downturn, too.

It was the start of a seven-year sales slide that would eventually undo the brewer altogether. But there was far more to the slide—for Leisy and all other local brewers—than the incorrect assumption that an up-ticking, post–World War II economy alone would help lift sales. Brewers anticipated more spending of discretionary income on beer, with or without advertising.

Leisy brewery president Herbert F. Leisy draws a mug of beer from the vat. *Courtesy of Cleveland Public Library.*

That didn't happen. In fact, despite the increased proliferation of larger national brands, sales of beer drastically declined, per capita, by 18 percent from 1947 to 1958. The downturn in sales and amplified competition was a one-two punch that left many brewers, including Leisy, reeling.

Partygoers pose for a photograph at Leisy Brewing Company's "Gay Nineties Rathskeller Party" at the Leisy Brewery in Cleveland. *Courtesy of Special Collections, Cleveland State University Archives.*

What's more, the competition at Standard, Cleveland-Sandusky and Pilsener in particular, had worked hard to curry favor with younger audiences via the mass media and ad campaigns. Leisy did almost the opposite, continuing to court to its traditional, older-skewing audience.

Company head Herbert F. Leisy (who took over the family business from Otto Leisy) eventually made some grand efforts to diversify his audience and lift slumping sales. The brewer repackaged its lagging Light Beer, in the hopes that a younger demographic would take note. It didn't.

Leisy also introduced Mello-Gold beer in 1955, thinking that perhaps a younger (and potentially female) audience would gravitate to a less bitter "premium" brew. The brand featured jingles by singer-pitchman Ray Charles, but the cost of the beer itself was a barrier to these as-yet untapped markets—and the patented "vacuum aging" process necessary to remove the bitterness was costly.

(The irony would come over twenty years later, when Miller Brewing Company of Milwaukee, Wisconsin, introduced the country to Miller Lite in

Brewmaster Carl Faller (left) Herbert F. Leisy (right) sample their new Leisy Brewing Company "Dortmunder Lager" in this 1939 *Cleveland Press* photo. *Courtesy of Special Collections, Cleveland State University Archives.*

grand fashion in 1975—a move that pushed many other large-scale brewers to introduce their own light beer brands and would inevitably change beer consumption history. Chronology, it seems, was working against Leisy and many other brewers of their time.)

There was also an attempt to stop the sales bleeding by wooing away Pilsener Brewing Company's George S. Carter and installing him as Leisy's new president. But the magic of his days at Pilsener didn't rematerialize.

There were other business missteps for Leisy, too, including a higher-alcohol Black Dallas Malt Liquor that never really generated a significant level of profit. It also introduced a robust Pilsner in 1958 that was critically hailed by Bavarian brewmasters at the Castle brewery but didn't fare well sales-wise, either.

Nothing seemed to stick. Like the industry as a whole, Leisy was late to identify ways to broaden beer's appeal outside of its already loyal, blue-collar, working-class audience. By the fall of 1959, Leisy closed its plant—originally as a "temporary measure for plant improvements," but it never reopened.

Leisy brands remained available to Cleveland beer drinkers until the mid-1960s, thanks to licensing and production by Canadian Ace Brewing in Chicago, Illinois. But Leisy, as Cleveland truly knew it, was no more.

CONSOLIDATION BECOMES THE STANDARD

On the surface of the "Fatal Fifties," Standard and its heritage Erin Brew brand seemed to be the most stable local concern—having experienced two multimillion-dollar expansion efforts that included a four-story brew and stock house, cold-storage and fermentation plants and, in 1950, a modern bottling/canning plant that brought its capacity to 550,000 barrels of beer annually.

At that commercial peak, the company employed more than four hundred people and had a five-state distribution footprint. And yet, by

Brewery workers inspect bottles of beer coming off the bottling line—ready for packaging and distribution—at the Standard Brewing Company. *Courtesy of Special Collections, Cleveland State University Archives.*

Cases of Pilsener Brewing Company's P.O.C. beer on the packing line. *Courtesy of Cleveland Public Library.*

1961, economic factors and a continuing downturn in Cleveland's economy and beer consumption led Standard to sell to the F.&M. Schaefer Brewing Company of New York—which was, at the time, the seventh-largest brewer nationally in terms of sales volume.

(A mere three years later, in 1964, Schaefer determined Cleveland operations to not be economically viable and sold the Train Avenue brewery to C. Schmidt and Sons, Inc.)

A view of the front entry of the C. Schmidt & Sons Brewery on the east side of Cleveland. *Courtesy of Special Collections, Cleveland State University Archives.*

Duquesne Brewing Company of Pittsburgh bought the beleaguered Pilsener Brewing Company in 1963 and produced P.O.C. (altering the abbreviation's meaning to "Pleasure on Call") for a decade until it went out of business in 1973. Duquesne sold the P.O.C. label (and others) to Schmidt, thereby allowing P.O.C. to be produced again in Cleveland.

Cleveland-Sandusky, like Leisy, struggled to identify new markets, even reviving its New York Special Brew that dated back to Prohibition, but the company never found its footing and by 1956 had controlling interest acquired by Marvin Bilsky, who had arrived at C-S only a year before, hired as vice-president and general manager.

Bilsky had a consumer background (his family ran a wholesale bakery operation) and worked hard to rebuild the organization—going so far as to revive the Crystal Rock brand. He created more appealing promotions of the Gold Bond beer and also purchased the brewing equipment and resources of Bellville, Illinois Star-Peerless Brewing Company in 1959.

His moves helped the company initially, but by 1962, C-S ceased operations and had arranged for a Detroit, Michigan brewer to continue producing its

A painted plaster statue-mascot of "Oscar" from the Cleveland-Sandusky Brewing Company. Oscar's image is noted as having advertised Gold Bond and Crystal Rock brands of beer. *Courtesy of Special Collections, Cleveland State University Archives.*

brands while retaining the distribution rights. It was a move eerily similar to Leisy's, which would come a short time later.

Back in 1944, Brewing Corporation of America had acquired Cleveland's Tip Top and Forest City breweries, which had increased its capacity to 1 million barrels annually. It positioned the corporation well for a controlling interest sale to Canadian Breweries, Ltd., which did business in America

Employees of Carling gather outside of the brewery to celebrate production goals for Black Label beer made in Cleveland. *Courtesy of Special Collections, Cleveland State University Archives.*

as Carling Brewing Company, nearly a decade later. The move kept the brewery alive longer than many contemporaries.

The former Carling was quite successful in pivoting when it needed to in order to be more successful as a business during the "Fatal Fifties"—the move to eliminate cone-top cans in favor of flat-top was particularly helpful in making them more appealing for retail outlets. When many other brewers were

Cleveland Cartage Company hoisted 120 big beer tanks at Carling's 9400 Quincy Avenue facility during a 1950s renovation and expansion. The glass-lined tanks each weighed more than sixteen tons and were forty-six feet long and approximately twelve feet in diameter. *Courtesy of Special Collections, Cleveland State University Archives.*

struggling mightily to hold that 1950s market share, Carling's nine-brewery footprint was cranking out well over 5 million barrels in sales annually, and it was the fourth-largest brewer in the nation behind Anheuser-Busch, Schlitz and Falstaff.

Carling continued to operate from the Peerless plant in Cleveland, producing both Red Cap and Black Label beers for multi-state distribution

Above: Mabel, the wholesome face of Carling's Black Label Beer. The "Mabel, Black Label," ad campaign is well remembered locally. *Courtesy of Carl H. Miller.*

Right: Carling Brewing introduced a "two-way 'Twist Cap'" advertising campaign, trumpeting the brewer's new packaging technology developed by Armstrong Cork Co. *Courtesy of Special Collections, Cleveland State University Archives.*

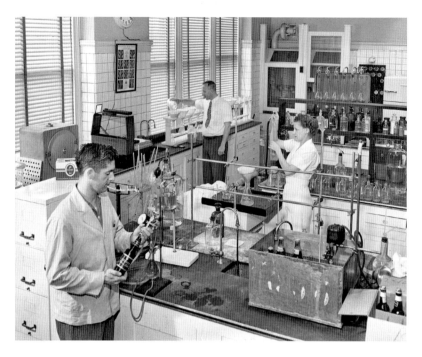

The Carling brewery quality control lab in action, where process improvements through science came to fore. *Courtesy of Special Collections, Cleveland State University.*

from Cleveland—although as time went on, the focus trained heavily on Black Label due to its popularity and price point. Black Label kept the company viable into the mid-1960s, when a new awareness of profitability made the brewer question its overhead. Carling carried on in Cleveland until 1971, when it was determined that continued business in the city was untenable (under the guise that Cleveland's plant was outmoded) and closed.

As fate would have it, Schmidt would acquire and utilize the Brewing Corp./Carling's Peerless location. The old plant was hardly outmoded. In fact, Schmidt management decided it was the perfect opportunity for them to expand operations, and the move positioned them to push output to 3 million barrels of annual beer production.

It remained Schmidt's headquarters until 1984, when the financially troubled Philadelphia brewer became the last of Cleveland's beer production operations to close. It was the first time in 150 years that Cleveland was without a brewery, but in a way, true Cleveland brewing ended in 1964; by then, all of Cleveland's original breweries were no more.

Little did Clevelanders know that it was not to be that way for long…

Chapter 9
A NEW WAVE

CRAFT BEER ARRIVES IN CLEVELAND

It is hard to imagine when walking through the Ohio City neighborhood today, especially on a warm Saturday afternoon, when West Twenty-fifth Street teems with locals and tourists alike, and every restaurant and bar has its patio doors flung open, that this bustling entertainment district was once desolate and nearly abandoned, save for the age-old institutions of the West Side Market and St. Ignatius High School.

That, however, was precisely the environment that brothers Patrick and Daniel Conway entered into when they launched Great Lakes Brewing Company in 1988. The brewery's home, Market Avenue, is now a charming, cobbled side street lined with the awnings and sidewalk patios of both the brewpub and several neighboring restaurants. Back then, however, it was little more than an alleyway.

"Nothing was here," Pat Conway said in a 2013 *Plain Dealer* article celebrating the brewery's twenty-fifth anniversary. "This was a rough-and-tumble neighborhood—fights, homicides. We were on an island down here, by ourselves."

It wasn't just the neighborhood that was uncharted territory for the Conways, though—the entire concept of a craft brewery was brand-new to Cleveland and only beginning to catch on across the rest of the country.

CLEVELAND BEER

A Movement Begins

Craft or microbreweries began to take hold in the United States starting around 1976, when Jack McAuliffe launched the short-lived but influential New Albion Brewing Company in Sonoma, California. McAuliffe, like many other pioneers in the industry, was bitten by the brewing bug after encountering the vast variety of beer styles available in Europe, which simply could not be found in the post-consolidation United States. Wanting to recreate those flavors at home, he began brewing his own take on British-style ales.

Other early entrants into the market, such as Sierra Nevada, followed suit and opened their doors in the ensuing years. The legalization of homebrewing in 1979 by President Jimmy Carter helped move the trend forward, and it wasn't long before many ambitious homebrewers considered offering their products on a commercial scale. Most of the early microbrewing action was centered on the coasts, however, and it would be some time before craft beer came to roost in the Midwest. Great Lakes had few precedents in the region (Bell's Brewing of Kalamazoo, Michigan, being a notable exception) when it opened its doors.

Great Lakes Gets Going

Like McAuliffe's, Pat Conway's beer inspiration came from a stint in Europe, having spent time in college at Loyola University's campus in Rome. During his time off, he traveled through Germany, England and Belgium, where he took in everything the pubs and beer gardens had to offer.

Upon returning home, he put himself through graduate school in Chicago by working as a bartender and noticed that American beer tastes were evolving—many of his customers requested imported styles that no domestic brewer was producing. After completing his degree, Conway worked a variety of jobs, from cab driver to schoolteacher, but was never really satisfied. Then, the idea of opening a brewery in his hometown struck.

"I looked under 'breweries' in the phone book," he said. "There were none, they were gone."

Pat's brother Dan, then just starting his career as a loan officer at Huntington Bank, offered to assist with start-up finances but became entangled in the business. He and Pat operate as co-CEOs with a 50/50 share of ownership.

The two incorporated the business in 1986 after toying with a number of names for their new concept, including Conway Brewing, North Coast Brewing and Western Reserve. Ultimately, though, the Great Lakes moniker spoke to them.

"It's one of the most recognizable geographic names in North America, if not the world," Pat said in an *Akron Beacon Journal* interview. "One-fifth of the fresh water is the Great Lakes. Seventy-five percent of the U.S. water is the Great Lakes."

The name, according to Dan Conway, also reflected the duo's ambitions to become a regional brewery.

It took the brothers two years to get the operation up and running. They signed a lease in 1987 on the first of several buildings the company would eventually come to occupy.

At the time, Cleveland was experiencing something of a rebirth— the Cleveland Browns were in the midst of several years of playoff runs (none of which, unfortunately, resulted in a Superbowl), a new downtown sports complex with an arena for the Cavaliers and ballpark for the Indians was in the works and the Flats had become a popular entertainment and nightlife destination. The Conways looked at sites in the Flats and just up the hill in the Warehouse District but ultimately settled on the unlikely Ohio City location, despite the misgivings of friends and family, because of the area's deep sense of history—the neighborhood had been home to many of the city's historic breweries, and the building that the brothers selected, itself, had an interesting background.

The storefront that was to become the brewpub had most recently housed the Market Street Exchange, a popular tavern and restaurant, but the building dated back to at least the 1860s, having started its life as Herman McClean's Feed and Seed store. It was later home to the Market Tavern, a popular hangout for local politicians during the 1930s, including Eliot Ness, who was Cleveland's safety director at the time. Great Lakes, as a company, likes to play up that history—one of its flagship beers, a Vienna lager, is named for Ness, and bartenders claim that a bullet lodged in the taproom's antique tiger mahogany bar came from Ness's gun—a novelty toy pistol flag reading "BANG!" protrudes from the bullet hole.

With a location selected, the Conways were ready to go, but there was just one problem. While the pair did not lack in vision and ambition, they were missing a very important skill—the actual ability to brew beer. Luckily for them, there were still a few veterans of the city's old school breweries around and willing to work. The brothers hired brewmaster Thaine Johnson and

The street view of the Great Lakes Brewing Company Patio at 2516 Market Avenue. *Courtesy of Great Lakes Brewing Co.*

engineer Charlie Price, two of the last brewers to work for C. Schmidt and Sons, to guide beer-making operations. While Price helped to source brewing equipment and design the brewhouse, Johnson developed the recipes that would come to be Great Lakes' small fleet of flagship beers.

Great Lakes Makes a Splash

The brewpub finally opened its doors on September 6, 1988, to a packed house of Clevelanders eager to sample the first beer brewed in the city in four years. Business has barely slowed down since then.

Great Lakes' arrival was widely trumpeted by the local media, with the *Plain Dealer* running a feature on the brewery a month before it opened and largely positive coverage (save for a few negative food reviews—it took the Conways some time to get the kitchen up to the same standard as the beer) continuing to flow over the next several years. Reporters, however, struggled at first to describe the concept to local audiences, lacking the language of craft beer that consumers now take for granted. The preview in the *Plain Dealer* explained the nascent craft beer scene this way: "Development of such micro-breweries to churn out private-label products for their own brew pubs is becoming a trend in other parts of the country in response to demands from upscale beer drinkers." Awkward reporting aside, the city embraced Great Lakes and its first two flagship beers, the aforementioned Eliot Ness amber lager and the Heisman (later renamed and much better known as Dortmunder Gold), almost immediately. The beers were easy-drinking and well crafted and, as lagers, represented styles not especially prevalent in the ale-heavy microbrew industry. Pat Conway puts it this way, "Dortmunder is the entryway into craft beers."

It didn't take long for the craft brewing community outside of Cleveland to take notice of Great Lakes, either. Only a year into operations, in 1990, the brewery took away the first of many medals it would win at the Great American Beer Festival. The Great American Beer Festival could accurately, but somewhat inadequately, be described as the Superbowl or Academy Awards of brewing—a huge annual conference and competition put on by the Brewers Association, the national trade organization for breweries. Although the competitors were far fewer in 1990 than now, it was something of a surprise to the more established brewers when Great Lakes won a gold medal in the Export/Specials category for Dortmunder (the Gold moniker was affixed to the brand in tribute to that award). It was a galvanizing moment for the infant brewery. "Pat called the staff together," Dan Conway said. "We were elated, high-fiving. It was uplifting."

The brewery would win another eleven medals over ensuing years.

"Going out to Denver and winning medals year after year, that was a really cool thing," said former brewmaster Andy Tveekrem, who took over the kettles after Johnson's retirement. "The Great American Beer Festival was largely a Colorado thing, and we'd win medals for porters and IPAs and pale ales, and guys would be like, 'Hey, what are you doing taking all our medals?'"

Edmund Fitzgerald Porter is the brewery's most decorated beer, having landed gold medals in 1991, 1993 and 2002 as well as a bronze in 2004 and silver in 2007.

The brewery's best known, and probably most beloved offering, however, is its winter seasonal, simply dubbed Christmas Ale. Spiced with a warming and aromatic mix of cinnamon, ginger and honey and clocking in at 7.5 percent ABV, Christmas Ale arrived on the scene in 1992 and has since

Salvaged relief work from the Schlather Brewing Company on display in Great Lakes Brewing Company's tasting room. *Courtesy of Great Lakes Brewing Co.*

developed a devoted cult following. Guests line up hundreds deep outside the brewery on Halloween for the first tapping of each year, and although it is only available for about two months, it accounts for 20 percent or more of the brewery's annual sales.

On the back of such popular and acclaimed beers, Great Lakes grew quickly in its early years, from brewing only 1,000 barrels in 1988 to topping 22,500 by 1999. The brewery's footprint expanded just as rapidly, first moving production into the neighboring Fries and Schuele building and, after outgrowing that space, into the last surviving structure of the old Schlather Brewing complex, a former storage and stable building two blocks away. The Conways had come a long way from hand-bottling beer and selling cases out of their mother's station wagon.

With Great Lakes having quickly established the viability of the brewpub concept in Northeast Ohio, it would be only a short time before other entrepreneurs followed the Conways' lead and opened their own microbreweries.

Chapter 10
SINK OR SWIM

CLEVELAND'S MICRO BOOM AND BUST

When Great Lakes Brewing Company first ventured into the marketplace in 1988, it was literally an open market for craft beer in Cleveland. However, by 1997, there were no fewer than six active craft breweries in the Cleveland area, including the Conway brothers' venture, and signs of a full-blown renaissance abounded. At that point, the brewery had gained some serious traction in the region and its success inspired a fair number of brewers, beer enthusiasts and, frankly, some various-and-sundry beer-related commercial entities to enter Cleveland and the surrounding suburbs' foamy fray.

Eager to cash in on the thirst for craft beer, national chains Rock Bottom and John Harvard's Brewhouse moved into the market and enjoyed moderate and modest attention, respectively.

The former opened in 1995 and spent over a decade as the anchor of the Old Powerhouse on Sycamore Street on the west bank of the Cleveland Flats. Rock Bottom brewed many varieties of beer with locally themed monikers—including a Dawg Pound Brown Ale named for Cleveland's NFL franchise—before yielding to market forces as the Flats role as a local nightlife hub declined and diminished in emphasis.

The latter (which closed and later reopened as the House of Brews) had a much shorter run by contrast—opening in 1997 and not quite stringing together three years between its two monikers in the old Customs House on the East Bank of the Cleveland Flats. Said market forces (and that shift away from the Flats) had a hand in its demise, too.

The Cleveland Chop House brewed beer for a time on West Saint Clair Avenue, as did the Northfield Park Microbrewery at Northfield's namesake harness-racing horse track. The Mad Crab Restaurant in Strongsville (which itself displaced the short-lived Melbourne Brewing Company) and Wallaby's, an Australian-themed microbrewery located in Westlake and, for a time, downtown Cleveland and Medina also entered and exited the scene in short order.

All merit a brief mention, given their place in the local brewing landscape of the time, although Wallaby's merits a special mention. It also did contract brewing under the Local Brewing Company name (on Sperry Road in Westlake) and had a hand in temporarily reviving the P.O.C. label, which spent roughly a year in retail stores before disappearing along with Local Brewing Company and the entire Wallaby's restaurant group.

However, there are four now-defunct brewers that had a significant impact on Cleveland's beer resurgence, and rather miraculously, two of them (as of this printing) are enjoying a second life in Cleveland's ever-changing brewing landscape.

CLEVELAND BREWING COMPANY: 1988–1994

Craig Chaitoff and David Lowman left their corporate lives behind when they formed the Cleveland Brewing Company. With an eye sharply trained on nostalgia—namely in resurrecting the Standard Brewing Company's famed Erin Brew label—they procured the financial backing of Edward Feighan, the great-grandson of Standard's co-founder John T. Feighan. The company would set up day-to-day operations (sans brewery) on Lakeside Avenue downtown.

With Feighan's help, the duo raised $420,000 in seed money for the business plan of returning Erin Brew to Cleveland. It didn't hurt that there were other fairly high-profile contributors; they included former Cuyahoga County commissioner Tim Hagan, Cleveland real estate developer James Carney and lawyer Bob Sweeney. All of them could readily identify with the idea of the Erin reboot—an idea that Chaitoff and Lowman had kicked around since their dorm room days at Miami University.

"People say Cleveland's experiencing a renaissance," the then twenty-year-old Chaitoff told United Press International. "But something was missing, and that was beer."

The new beer with a decidedly old-school name was instantly popular in the city and, over time, expanded distribution into much of northern Ohio. The beer even earned a silver medal at the 1989 Great American Beer Festival, in the European Amber category. It didn't even matter to locals that that the product itself was technically a contract-brew manufactured in nearby Pittsburgh, Pennsylvania, thanks to Clevelanders' heart-on-the-sleeve wistfulness for a bygone era.

Although Cleveland Brewing Company had entered the market with little competition, the brewing field quickly crowded after Great Lakes Brewing Company's arrival just months later in 1988. By 1994, the brewer had ceased producing Erin Brew and all pertinent operations.

CROOKED RIVER: 1994–2000

One beer brand that scored well with locals was Crooked River. Named in tribute to the Cuyahoga River's Iroquoian translation, the brewery flourished during its short lifespan before it disappeared "when the label wound up in bankruptcy," as Marc Bona of the *Cleveland Plain Dealer* noted in 2010.

After brewing its first batches in 1994, things appeared to be rolling along quite well for the brewery—it enjoyed the attention and support of the city fathers and the local professional sports franchises. During its tenure, Crooked River made a specialty beer for Cleveland's bicentennial (1996) and had featured brews at Jacobs Field (now Progressive Field, home of the Cleveland Indians) and Gund Arena (now Quicken Loans Arena, home of the Cleveland Cavaliers) and an "Expansion Draft," marking the return of Cleveland Browns football to the area. They also landed a fortuitous sponsorship package with the now-defunct Cleveland Grand Prix auto race.

Distribution was a challenge early on—when the company began expanding, it didn't have a sales force commensurate to its retail needs, so it signed with six different distributors. The move took a serious chunk of the company's financial returns.

Founder Stephen Danckers told *Small Business News* in 2002, "Gung ho enthusiasm and technique will only get you so far. At some point you need to make a profit. [We] didn't have business experience and know-how. It was always a search for money. Sometimes you'd just forget about it, but it was always there. Finally, it just caught up with us."

The defunct Crooked River Brewing Company on Center Street in the Flats. *Courtesy of Carl H. Miller.*

To wit, cash flow problems eventually took out the company at the knees. A business restructuring and acquisition by local impresario C. David Snyder in 1998 rescued the brewery from what seemed to be an inevitable Chapter 11 bankruptcy. But his $500,000 investment only served as a temporary fix. By 2000, Crooked River was no more.

Though the original company is long-since defunct, the labels live on and have had a bit of a renaissance, thanks to Jerome Welliver. His Black Box Brewing Company in Westlake is brewing the original recipes, with local beverage stores and both Giant Eagle and Heinen's grocery stores carrying his revivals of Crooked River's Settlers Ale, Lighthouse Gold Kolsch, Cool Mule Porter, Black Forest Lager and many other varieties.

Diamondback Brewery and Pub: 1996–2000

Timing, as they say, is everything. When the Diamondback Brewery and Pub opened on Prospect Avenue in the city's newly christened Gateway district, it had plenty to offer—namely a fifteen-barrel brewery nestled into a spacious yet cozy, multi-level dining room.

It was busy almost from the word "go," especially so when there were sporting or special events happening at Jacobs Field or Gund Arena. The

Indians were a powerhouse baseball franchise during this period, which kept *Cleveland Magazine*'s "Best New Restaurant for 1997" plenty busy during the summer months. But the pre–LeBron James version of the Cavaliers struggled mightily during that same timeframe, which made for a struggle business-wise during those long winter months.

Diamondback had a hearty slate of beers, including a Belgian dubbel, hefeweizen, gueuze-lambic and framboise, and its Hempen Roggen bested thirty-three different entries in the "Experimental Beer (Lager or Ale)" category as a gold medal winner in the 1999 Great American Beer Festival.

But despite the honor (along with menu tweaks, increased happy hours and other adjustments), the brewery closed the following year. An attempt to resuscitate the location as Barons Brewpub, though well meaning, didn't pan out. It closed again months after opening.

Western Reserve: 1997–2002

Co-founded by CEO Gavin Smith and brewer Andrew Craze, Western Reserve had a short but impactful run as an independent brewer in the Cleveland area. With headquarters located in the Midtown section of Cleveland, the duo also hit their apex in 1999, when Western Reserve's summer seasonal beer Cloud Nine (a citrusy Belgian white) was awarded a silver medal in the "Belgian and French Style Specialty Ales" category at that year's Great American Beer Festival.

As it turned out, 1999 was an especially good year for current and former Cleveland brewers, with GABF medals being awarded to mainstays Great Lakes Brewing Company and Willoughby Brewing Company as well.

Things went south a short time later. While sales, kudos and production continued to increase with each year, they never reached the levels that Craze and Smith imagined. But something else was increasing too: the company's debts.

The debts weren't financial alone. Wary of signing into a distribution contract with one of the city's big names, Craze and Smith did their own distribution—and it was the ultimate time management killer. As Cleveland's *Scene* magazine noted, "For consumers, it was sometimes easier to find a Western Reserve in Columbus than it was in Lakewood."

At some point around 2000, the financial debts became overwhelming enough that the company started looking for a buyer. When that option failed, the duo opted for Chapter 7 bankruptcy—a total liquidation of the brewery assets. At one point, Craze told *Scene* that he had attempted to gain access to the brewery during that time, but the bankruptcy court's trustees had changed the locks.

Western Reserve produced a number of other varieties (Bockzilla bock, American Wheat, Nut Brown, Lake Effect Winter Ale and Twist & Stout). But the company's attempts to become profitable were unsuccessful when faced with increasing competition, and by early 2002, the brewery had shuttered its doors.

Some of Western Reserve's recipes—including Bockzilla and Cloud Nine—are now also being brewed intermittently by Black Box's Welliver.

Staying Afloat: Survivors of the 1990s Beer Boom

Not every brewery that entered the local market in the ten years following the arrival of Great Lakes Brewing Company shared the sad fates of Crooked River, Diamondback, Western Reserve and their contemporaries. While breweries located within the city generally did not fare well during that time period, some of those that took root in the suburbs not only survived but also flourished.

The Brew Kettle

One of the first breweries to make a lasting impact in the outer rings of the metropolitan area was the Brew Kettle. Launched in 1995, the Brew Kettle succeeded not just because of the quality of its beer but also because of its unique business model. In addition to operating a brewpub and restaurant, the Brew Kettle is also one of the only local brewhouses to feature a brew-on-premise.

Brew-on-premise (BOP) operations allow guests who are curious about the brewing process an opportunity to learn how to make beer, hands-on, without making the investment in an entire home-brewing set up or dealing with the potential mess that an errant batch of wort could create in the kitchen. Brew-on-premise customers select a beer style (Brew Kettle currently offers approximately eighty varieties) and are paired with a professional brewer, who provides the ingredients and oversees them as they make a batch of beer on small (approximately half-barrel) kettles. The professional oversight assures that the customer correctly follows the recipe. After the active part of the brewing process is complete, the brew-on-premise ferments the beer. Customers return when the beer is ready to bottle and take their creations home. The entire process costs a bit more than brewing at home, but guests view it as a social activity and often brew in collaboration with friends. Many customers return regularly to brew additional beers.

Even though the Brew Kettle will celebrate its twentieth anniversary this year, the BOP continues to be booked months in advance—would-be brewers looking for a Saturday afternoon brew time (the most popular time slot) are often obliged to wait up to six months for an appointment.

Founder and opening brewmaster Chris McKim was first introduced to the brew-on-premise concept in 1994 while on vacation in Costa Rica, when he overheard some fellow holiday-makers from Vancouver, Canada, discussing their local BOP. McKim, a homebrewer, was intrigued and ended up visiting that Canadian operation several times to test out the idea before deciding it was something he could do at home. He opened the Brew Kettle in a nondescript Strongsville strip mall a year later, starting, at the same time, his Ringneck Brewing Company, which marketed the brewpub's beers to other outlets. The two names caused confusion, and the Ringneck brand was eventually abandoned. The brewery's flagship beers, including 4 C's Pale Ale, White Rajah IPA and Black Rajah Black IPA, as well as seasonal offerings, are distributed today under the Brew Kettle name.

Over the past twenty years, the Brew Kettle has expanded at least seven times, adding a separate production brewery in a warehouse about a mile south of the brewpub in 2007 and growing the pub itself to encompass several additional storefronts in its building by 2010. A winemaking arm of the business, dubbed Your Wine Cellar, made its debut around the same time.

Initial output at the production works was about 2,500 barrels a year, but through subsequent additions and expansions, including a new bottling line, capacity increased to 5,000 barrels by 2012. More recent upgrades should bring capacity to 10,000 barrels per annum. The expansions have helped the brewery keep up with demand—just barely. "We sell it literally as fast as we can make it," McKim said.

In March 2013, Brew Kettle entered into an ownership agreement with an investment group, headed by Chris Russo, best known locally as a partner in the Panini's chain of sports bars. Under the new structure, Russo and his partners were to run the restaurant and brewpub, while McKim would continue to oversee the production brewery. Just a few months later, however, McKim retired, handing the reins of the brewhouse over to brewmaster Jack Kephart, who joined the company in 2007, after a stint at Willoughby Brewing Company. The transition has seemingly been smooth, with the restaurant and brew-on-premise remaining extremely popular, and the brewery continuing to expand its distribution footprint and offerings.

BUCKEYE BREWING COMPANY

Garin Wright entered into the beer business in 1997 having never brewed a batch. When his father and Buckeye co-owner, Robert, floated the idea of opening a brewery, Garin simply quit his day job and learned how to brew on the fly.

"I just dug in and learned it all on my own," he said in a *Cleveland Magazine* feature. "To really understand the business, that's the only way to do it. It's all about repetition. The more batches you brew, the better you become. It's that simple."

The Wrights started their operation in the southeast suburb of Bedford Heights as a brew-on-premise, known as the Brew Keeper, and Buckeye Brewing, which functioned as the production brewery. In 2006, they sold the Brew Keeper arm of the company. The new owners relocated Brew Keeper to North Ridgeville, where it briefly enjoyed success as a brewpub and BOP but folded in 2010.

The Wrights had bigger plans anyway. They moved Buckeye Brewing into an enormous old rayon factory on Walford Avenue on Cleveland's west side in 2006 and shortly thereafter opened up the Buckeye Beer Engine, one of the area's first great craft beer bars, in the west side suburb of Lakewood. Named for the fact that two of its draft offerings are pulled from hand-pumped beer casks, the Beer Engine sells a number of Buckeye beers alongside a well-curated list of about twenty drafts from craft breweries all over the United States and the world and boasts one of the most extensive bottle lists around. The Beer Engine regularly hosts tasting event with big-name craft breweries and also hosts a number of themed beer festivals, including the 420 Hop Fest, a weekend-long April event devoted to IPAs and weedy innuendo.

At the production facility, the Wrights brew on a fifteen-barrel system, putting out around one thousand barrels a year. While some of that beer is kegged and distributed locally and at the Beer Engine, most of it is sold in twenty-two-ounce bomber bottles. The production facility is not open to the public.

The names of Buckeye's beers reflect Garin's belief that they should be short and memorable, hence titles like Hippie IPA, Martian Marzen and Madison Kolsch.

Garin is something of an iconoclast and always outspoken with his opinions. In Cleveland, a city that loves spiced Christmas beers in the style of Great Lakes' Christmas Ale, he chooses to instead brew a Belgian golden ale, known as Christmas Girl, as his holiday seasonal; when LeBron James made his infamous decision to leave the Cavaliers in 2010, Wright parodied the basketballer's "Witness" slogan with a beer called "Witless," attracting a good deal of publicity for the Belgian-style witbier in the process.

WILLOUGHBY BREWING COMPANY

Located about twenty-five miles east of downtown Cleveland, the Lake County suburb of Willoughby boasts a charming downtown that seemed like a natural fit for a brewpub to young entrepreneur T.J. Reagan. The fact that there was vacant, yet spectacular, old rail car repair shop located just off the main drag didn't hurt either. After spending nearly two years and more than $1 million on equipment and renovations to the impressive brick structure, Reagan opened Willoughby Brewing Company in early 1998.

The brewery quickly became a mainstay of the area's restaurant scene and, like many of its area contemporaries, won acclaim early on for its original beers. Its Railway Razz, a raspberry-infused wheat beer, took away a GABF silver medal in 1999 and bronze in 2000 and 2001. Saison L'Ete, a Belgian farmhouse ale, also won silver in 2000. Despite several changes of personnel in the brewhouse, Willoughby continues to produce Railway Razz. It was the brewery's second head brewer, Jason Sims, though, who created what is now probably its best known offering, Peanut Butter Cup Coffee Porter, a rich, dark ale infused with peanut butter-flavored coffee beans from a local roaster. Peanut Butter Cup Coffee Porter won a gold medal in the Specialty Beer category at the 2014 World Beer Cup.

The company changed hands in 2011, with a new ownership group of Jeremy Van Horn, Nika McNulty and Bobby George taking Reagan's place and upgrading much of the brewery's infrastructure, including draft lines and pumps. The original brewhouse, with its fifteen-barrel copper kettles remained, but Sims left, and for a few years, the leadership of the brew team fluctuated. The situation has since stabilized under brewmaster Rick Seibt, a former homebrewer who made the jump into professional brewing. Seibt continues to brew the Willoughby classics that the people of Lake County and Cleveland as a whole have come to love but is also innovating, adding more West Coast–style IPAs and Belgian-inspired selections to the tap list.

ROCKY RIVER BREWING COMPANY

You could scarcely design a more archetypal Cleveland brewpub than Rocky River Brewing Company. It has everything most people have come to expect in a local microbrewery. Dark wood fixtures and worn brass rails? Check. Shiny copper kettles housed behind glass? Check. Framed historical photos? Of course. And a wall of fame, bedecked with framed medals? Absolutely.

The last item on that list is largely courtesy of the brewmaster hired by owners Bob and Gary Cintron when they opened their brewpub in its namesake suburb back in 1998. Of all the people brewing beer in Greater Cleveland, few, if any, are as decorated as Matt Cole. Cole has since moved on to Fat Heads, but the reputation he built at Rocky River, and quite a few of his recipes, remain.

Like Garin Wright at Buckeye, the Cintron brothers had no experience with brewing when they opened the pub, although they had plenty of restaurant experience. A research trip to Great Lakes Brewing Company led them to Cole, who was working there as the pub brewer at the time.

Set free to experiment, Cole racked up an impressive thirteen GABF medals at Rocky River from 1998 to 2008, including a gold his very first year for Bearbottom Stout, an Irish dry stout. An additional four medals from the World Beer Cup and numerous local and regional awards round out Rocky River's impressive slate of accolades.

Cole's replacement, Jim Lieb, has continued Rocky River's tradition of mixing it up. The brewery's three flagships are all very light, approachable beers—a blonde, a Kolsch and a blueberry ale—this allows the brewmaster the freedom to try out new recipes to satisfy customers' tastes for darker, more bitter or just more challenging beers.

Unlike many of their Cleveland colleagues, the Cintrons do not have designs on expansion. They have no interest in getting into the fray of bottling or canning and distributing their beers. They are happy with the size and footprint of their establishment and seem to know every regular who comes through the doors. In that respect, Rocky River is like the corner saloon of old—a neighborhood gathering place—this one just happens to make its own beer.

Another notable, if farther-flung, brewery that opened in this time period was Ohio Brewing Company, which arrived in Niles in 1997 but did not last long. Owners Chris and Michael Verich tried again in 2008 with two Akron brewpubs but again overextended themselves. Sporadic periods of production brewing followed, starting in 2010, but by 2014, they had given up and sold off their equipment. In 2015, however, reports surfaced locally that the Verichs were seeking to relaunch the brand.

Contrastingly, Akron neighbor Thirsty Dog Brewing Company cycled through a few business models before hitting runaway success. The company first opened as a brewpub in 1997 and added satellite locations over the next few years. In 2003, the company began contract brewing for other concerns and by 2005 had closed its pubs. In 2007, owner John Najeway moved operations into the historic Burkhart Brewing Company building in downtown Akron and resumed brewing Thirsty Dog beers in earnest. The brewery is best known for its Old Leghumper Porter and its 12 Dogs of Christmas Ale, which many Clevelanders claim is better than Great Lakes' beloved holiday brew. Thirsty Dog brewmaster Tim Rastetter, who previously served as an assistant brewer at Great Lakes, had a hand in developing the original Christmas Ale recipe.

Chapter 11

THE INAUSPICIOUS AUGHTS

A would-be brewer considering going into business in Cleveland in the first few years of the new century could be forgiven for being cautious given the shake-ups in the local market over the previous decade. While Great Lakes and a few other concerns were thriving, many other breweries had risen precipitously, only to crash. Compounding the problem, starting in 2001 was the post-9/11 recession and banking crisis that plunged the nation into an economic quagmire for the better part of a decade. Cleveland was especially hard-hit by the dip in the economy—businesses failed frequently, and predatory lending practices led many home and business owners into foreclosure.

Only one new local brewery opened in the first years of the 2000s—the Quarryman in Berea, and it only lasted about three years after its 2001 opening. But it was soon replaced by the first of a handful of humble breweries that would dare to open their doors in what could otherwise be called an indifferent (at best) economic climate.

CORNERSTONE BREWING COMPANY

It was only a matter of time after the Quarryman closed its doors that a new brewery would take over its space. It was a perfect fit for a brewpub—located on the quaint town square of Berea, a suburb home to Baldwin-

Wallace College and the Cleveland Browns training facility. The long, narrow storefront was charmingly appointed with an old-meets-new vibe courtesy of worn wood floors, exposed ductwork, an open kitchen and lofty back bar, wood-burning iron stove and gleaming black granite countertops. The fact that the brew system was already in place was also helpful. It was pretty much "plug in and play" when owner Roy Blalock acquired the keys in 2004.

Cornerstone's first brewmaster was Erik Rothschiller, who picked up a homebrewing hobby during a stint in the military. Jay Cox joined him in the brewhouse in 2006; ever self-effacing, Cox went on to become the sole brewer but refuses to identify himself as a "brewmaster."

The brewery features three flagship beers: Grindstone Gold, a pale lager; Sandstone, a Marzen or Oktoberfest-style amber lager; and Seven, an ever-evolving India Pale Ale. The names of the beers and that of the brewery itself reference Berea's role as a quarrying town—Berea sandstone helped to build the city of Cleveland.

Since Cornerstone does not carry "guest" beers, Cox has free rein to brew seasonal and experimental beers as he pleases to keep the brewery's draft lines flowing. His popular pumpkin beer, Linus' Revenge, is a fall favorite, while Rowan, a Scotch ale lands on tap every January in honor of the legendary poet Robert Burns' birthday.

Cox's penchant for experimentation led him to create what he believes might have been one of the first black IPAs or Cascadian dark ales in the country, back in 2006, well before the style gained national traction. He blended an IPA with a porter in kegs to achieve the style's distinct blend of hop bite and dark, roasty malt character. He now brews a beer called Evil Entity X that is darkened not by heavily kilned malt but by sinamar, an extract that deepens the color of a beer without significantly altering the flavor. He told *Akron Beacon Journal* reporter Rick Armon that he likes to see how the beer's color alters people's perception of the flavor.

"I'd get the people who'd say, 'Wow, this is really roasty,' and the what-not. Only I knew. So now I make it with as little roast as I can get in a beer, but as black as I can get it. It's my favorite."

Cornerstone made its first foray into outside distribution in 2015, canning its popular Erie Blu, a wheat ale infused with blackberries and raspberries, for sales at Cleveland Browns Stadium.

BLACK BOX BREWING COMPANY

Jerome Welliver, owner/brewmaster at Black Box Brewing in Westlake, took the road less traveled when he opened his brewery in 2006. Forgoing the tried-and-true brewpub model, Welliver instead chose to open a small production works, sans taproom. His beers are available only for retail sale off-premise—in other words, they have to speak for themselves.

Welliver said he "went the harder route than most craft brewers, who usually start with a taphouse and expand…But for all the long, eighteen-hour days, we've been really successful and stayed plenty busy."

Welliver's entrée into brewing came almost by accident. He purchased the winemaking and homebrew shop J.W. Dover that houses Black Box in 1997, almost on a whim. He was a regular customer prior to buying the shop and stumbled on the opportunity to take over during a conversation with the previous owner. He stumbled on his brewhouse in much the same way, buying the equipment used from a defunct Mansfield brewpub after a friend spotted a "brewery for sale" sign. The equipment sat around in his garage for several years until he was able to secure funding to launch the brewery.

Outside of his inspired Crooked River and Western Reserve revival, Welliver brews a fair number of his own original Black Box brews, including Plumber's Crack amber ale and Triple Cherry Delite, a Belgian tripel-style fortified with cherries.

For years, he also co-hosted *Beer Talk Radio* on WERE-AM 1300 with Jack Curtis and Larry "Eddy" Adkinson, talking all things beer.

"Because of that show, I got to be friends with almost every single brewer in Cleveland," Welliver said. "It was a great time to be immersed in the business. Anyone who had something to show, to taste, they came on and we became friends."

Among those people were Craze of Western Reserve and Crooked River's Danckers.

"I was with them all when first tastings happened and when the kosher blessings were made at Western Reserve…I saw all of that American craft beer revolution in the first-person in Cleveland. It was a big part of my life and that's how I found my way to brewing itself."

Welliver said that while everyone was "hammering these beers with over-the-top spice, over-the-top-hops, everything they could cram into a beer," he felt that "Western Reserve and Crooked River both had a repertoire that was more sessionable," and that was a big part of what interested him in bringing them back.

"When you're in the craft brewing business, any way you can fill your fermenters and keep offering product is a good thing, because it also makes money. And I'll say that it was more than just labels purchased—when we did Western Reserve, we had Andy Craze involved in the brewing process to ensure that our process was yielding a beer that was exactly like their old system produced," he said.

"Same thing with Danckers, who we also brewed multiple batches with…It's more than a marketing tool; I didn't want to just bring back the name. Anyone can do that. I wanted to bring back the beer. That's what was important to me. And we've won awards for doing exactly that."

As of press time, Welliver's Black Box and Crooked River (Settler's Ale) wares are being served at Progressive Field during Cleveland Indians games, and his revival of the Crooked River Yuletide Ale is starting to pick up speed in a city that loves holiday beer. He estimates his overall production of all beer at Black Box (including the heritage revivals) is "somewhere around 1,100–1,200 barrels annually."

"We're happy where we are," he says. "We're fortunate. We're selling as much beer as we can make."

INDIGO IMP BREWERY

Matt Chappel does not do things like everybody else. From its very beginnings until its closing in the summer of 2015, his Indigo Imp Brewery trod its own path in every way, from its packaging to its tasting room and right down to how the beer was made.

Opened in 2008, Indigo Imp immediately set itself apart from the rest of the local brewery scene by employing open fermentation to make its beers. For most brewers, the process of beer making follows the same route—mashing the grain, boiling the wort, cooling the wort and moving it to a sealed fermenter tank where yeast is added. The yeast variety is carefully chosen for the flavor properties it will impart, and the temperature of the fermenter is monitored and programmed to ensure that the liquid within stays at just the right temperature for that particular yeast strain to work most efficiently. Chappel's method started the same, but when it came time to ferment the wort, he let nature take its course—all of Indigo Imp's beers were fermented in open vats, and while he did pitch some commercial yeast into his brew, he also left the brewery's windows open to allow the naturally occurring yeasts in the air to get into the liquid and play a role in fermentation.

As Chappel often explained to tour groups and guests visiting his tasting room, open fermentation is how all beer used to be made prior to modern understanding of microbiology, and it remains in use in many breweries in Belgium. He said that Indigo Imp was able to achieve a consistent product, despite the vagaries of the wild yeasts.

Like Black Box, Indigo Imp was primarily a production brewery, with the better part of its output being bottled in six-packs and sold in a limited distribution radius around northern Ohio. The beer was unfiltered and bottle-conditioned. One bottle in each six-pack, nicknamed the "Imp Bottle" had its neck dipped in brightly colored wax—just another visual touch to set it apart. Each Imp variety had a specific color of wax assigned to it—the flagship Blonde Bombshell featured royal blue wax, while Jester Pale Ale had red, and so on.

Located in Tyler Village, a redeveloped elevator factory in Cleveland's emerging Midtown neighborhood, Indigo Imp's small warehouse brewery was only open to the public on Friday afternoons. Guests visiting during those brief hours got to chat directly with Chappel and his wife, Kathy, the brewery's only other employee.

In keeping with Chappel's "different is better" approach to everything beer-related, all of Indigo Imp's taproom exclusive offerings were pulled from naturally carbonated casks that are kept at cellar temperature. The tasting room and the brewery itself offered further, quirky evidence of Chappel's love of tinkering—the brewing equipment, visible from the bar, was made from repurposed dairy tanks. The bar itself was made of old pallet wood, hand built, along with several high-top tables and an Astroturf-lined bocce ball court, by Chappel himself.

Doing things oneself, by hand, and on a small scale, was how Indigo Imp operated and was likely a contributing factor in its closing. Chappel quietly ceased distributing beer in early 2015 and by July announced the brewery's closing. He said operating Indigo Imp was no longer a priority for him and that he wanted to be able to spend more time with his family. Indigo Imp represented the first local brewery closing since Rock Bottom shut its doors in 2006.

SLOW AND STEADY: GREAT LAKES GROWS CAUTIOUSLY

Although the early 2000s may not have brought a flood of new breweries into the area, the city's largest brewery continued to enjoy great success both locally and in an ever-expanding distribution radius. At the same time, the company solidified its philosophy of environmental stewardship and expanded its philanthropic efforts.

The fermenters at Great Lakes Brewing Company are the largest in the city. *Photo by Leslie Basalla.*

In 2001, Great Lakes hosted its first annual Burning River Fest. The name of the weekend-long outdoor music, beer and ecology festival, which takes place at Whiskey Island, refers to an infamous incident in 1969 in which the severely polluted Cuyahoga River caught fire. The burning of the river raised a nationwide alarm about water pollution and led directly to the passage of the Clean Water Act of 1972. Another of the brewery's flagships, Burning River Pale Ale, derives its name from the ignominious incident. Great Lakes Brewing Company, itself, having taken its name from the region's greatest natural resource, is serious about keeping waterways clean. Proceeds from the festival benefit its Burning River Foundation.

Said Pat Conway of the lakes, "It's our Yosemite; it's our Grand Canyon."

In addition to the charitable festival, Great Lakes Brewing's other sustainability efforts include vermicomposting all of the restaurant's food scraps, offering its spent brewing grain to local farmers for feed and even pulling in frigid outdoor air during the winter keep the brewery's coolers cold. The brewery's delivery trucks, as well as its iconic "Fatty Wagon," a bus that shuttles visitors from the brewery to Cleveland Indians home games, are fueled with spent cooking oil from the brewpub's fryers.

These sustainability efforts tie into what the Conways call Great Lakes' "triple bottom line." The company strives for financial success, engagement with the community and environmental stewardship. The philosophy is represented in the brewery's logo by three wavy water lines.

Throughout the 2000s, Great Lakes slowly increased its output and distribution, reaching thirteen states by 2010. "We've been careful and patient," Pat Conway said. "We don't want to compromise our quality."

While emerging as a regional brewing powerhouse, Great Lakes also continued to take its role as an anchor of the Ohio City neighborhood seriously. Building on the momentum of the brewpub, a growing number of bars and restaurants, including the Flying Fig, McNulty's Bier Markt and the Old Angle, began doing business in the area between 1999 and 2006. "We continue to grow because of the quality of our product, and we're benefitting from the growth of the area and the surrounding restaurants," Conway said.

In addition to increasing its output, Great Lakes also continued to introduce new beers that would become part of its seasonal line up. Nosferatu, an American Strong Ale, arrived in 2001, and in 2003, on the heels of a massive August blackout that left Cleveland and much of the eastern United State in darkness, came Blackout Stout, a massive, 9 percent ABV Russian Imperial Stout.

The Great Lakes Brewing Company's brewhouse wall and grain silos. *Photo by Leslie Basalla.*

By decade's end, Great Lakes was poised to kick off a $7 million capital improvement project that would again increase its capacity and continue to transform its Ohio City location. That level of optimism and ambition was soon to be reflected by a new crop of breweries arriving in the city.

Chapter 12
MAKING WAVES

NEW MOMENTUM FOR LOCAL BEER

FAT HEADS BREWERY

Prior to his stints at Baltimore Brewing and Great Lakes, and his award-winning days at Rocky River Brewing Company, brewmaster Matt Cole was just another college kid in Pittsburgh, Pennsylvania, with a thirst for beer and a big appetite, which he often slaked at a South Side bar and restaurant called Fat Heads, where the only things bigger than the beer selection were the enormous sandwiches.

"It was a great place to hang out, if you could get a seat," Cole said in a *Plain Dealer* interview.

When he began to consider opening his own brewery, that favorite old watering hole sprung into Cole's mind, and he made a trip back to Pittsburgh to see if he could get Fat Heads owner Glenn Benigni on board. Even though he almost lost his nerve and nearly turned back about ten miles outside of Pittsburgh, Cole regained his composure and must have had a good proposal, as Benigni and several other investors joined him in opening Fat Heads Brewery and Saloon in North Olmsted in 2009.

The brewery's building, a former greengrocer called Danny Boy Farm Market, had sat vacant for a few years but had long been on Cole's mind. When he would shop for produce there, he often thought, "This would be a great place for a brewery."

The new brewpub quickly became a case of history repeating itself. Like the Pittsburgh original, the location was a huge success, and despite its spacious footprint, with a forty-seat bar and room for about two hundred additional guests, weekends often brought long waits to be seated. Between the beer consumed on premise and the kegs shipped to Pittsburgh, Cole could barely brew fast enough to keep up with demand. And like his creations at previous gig, Rocky River, Cole's brews began racking up accolades almost immediately.

In 2009, Up in Smoke, a smoked porter, won a silver medal at GABF. In 2010, Fat Heads flagship IPA, Head Hunter, an eighty-seven IBU West Coast–style hop bomb, took a silver in the American style IPA category. It won the bronze the following year. The year 2011 also saw Battle Axe Baltic Porter walking away with a gold medal. In fact, Fat Heads has won at least one GABF medal every year since opening. The brewery also has four World Beer Cup silver medals to its credit and numerous awards from local and regional beer festivals.

Given the brewery's outstanding reputation and the fact that it was already distributing Head Hunter and its other flagship beer, Bumbleberry, a blueberry wheat ale, in kegs and bottles, an expansion was necessary by 2012. In March of that year, Fat Heads took over a warehouse in Middleburg Heights and installed a 25-barrel brew system, purchased used from Harrisburg, Pennsylvania's Troegs Brewery. Initial capacity at the new production brewery was about 7,500 barrels, but continuing increases in tank space allowed it to hit 12,000 barrels by the end of the year.

In early 2013, Fat Heads opened a taproom within the production brewery. While it remains something of a best-kept secret, compared to the perpetually packed brewpub, the Taphouse at Fat Heads is becoming an increasingly popular destination for area beer drinkers and tourists alike, who get to marvel at the brewery's massive 120-barrel fermenters, only a few yards away from the reclaimed bowling alley bar.

"There is no separation whatsoever," Cole told *Cleveland Scene*'s Douglas Trattner. "You're basically going to be right in the thick of a working brewery. You'll see it, you'll hear it, you'll smell it."

As if that level of contact with the process wasn't enough, Cole noted another advantage to quaffing a pint or two in the taproom. "Beer is always freshest at the source."

Alongside the beer and a limited menu of food, the Taphouse offers live music on weekends, often something with a hippie bent, leaning toward classic acoustic rock, folk, reggae and Grateful Dead covers. Eschewing the local tradition of naming beers after Cleveland landmarks and historical figures, Cole's beer names tend to reflect his taste in music—several, including Jack

Straw pilsner, Shakedown Stout and Sunshine Daydream session IPA, make direct references to Grateful Dead songs or albums; others, like Hippy Sippy stout, Up in Smoke porter, and Head Trip Belgian tripel cheekily allude to other facets of hippie culture.

In addition to being on the forefront of what would over the next few years become something of a local taproom revolution, Fat Heads has innovated in other ways. It was one of the first local breweries to regularly offer some of its beer in cans. Trail Head, a fresh-hopped pale ale, arrived in canned six-packs in the summer of 2014, followed that fall by the brief appearance of four-packs of Hop Stalker, a fresh-hopped IPA.

Like Great Lakes, Fat Heads also puts it money where its mouth is when it comes to supporting its favorite causes. A portion of the proceeds from sales of Trail Head benefits the Cleveland Metroparks Trails Fund, helping the local park system to maintain, rehabilitate and expand its 270 miles of hiking and bike trails. Fat Heads has also brewed special beers to benefit breast cancer and ALS research.

Fat Heads rapid growth and ambitious expansions mirrored the increasing popularity of craft beer both locally and nationwide. With interest in locally made beer clearly on the rise, a wave of new breweries, some with aspirations just as grand as Cole's, started to flow into the local scene.

MARKET GARDEN BREWERY

The buzz began building around Ohio City sometime in 2009. What was Sam McNulty up to now? The affable entrepreneur was already a well-known and highly recognizable figure in the neighborhood, having launched the popular Belgian beer bar Bier Markt in 2005, followed by Italian wine bar/restaurant Bar Cento in 2007 and Prohibition-themed, subterranean cocktail lounge Speakeasy in 2009. Armed with a degree in urban studies and possessed with an almost-evangelical enthusiasm for the neighborhood, McNulty and his establishments had already helped to change the face of West Twenty-fifth Street. When construction fences began to rise around a long-abandoned Middle Eastern grocery store and adjacent poultry slaughterhouse next to the West Side Market, observers knew that McNulty's next move would be a big one. By the beginning of 2010, plans for Market Garden Brewery were on the public's radar.

It would be another year and a half before Market Garden Brewery finally opened in June 2011, on the heels of a complex and expensive build out.

The final product was an expansive brewpub with three ground-level dining spaces and the brewhouse in back forming a C-shape around an eighty-seat outdoor beer garden, replete with communal tables, locust trees and a massive wood-burning fireplace.

Plying the brew kettles was Andy Tveekrem, a galvanizing figure in the Cleveland beer scene, who, after a decade away, had returned home. Tveekrem was a founding member of the Society of Northern Ohio Brewers (SNOBs) homebrew club and had talked his way into a job at Great Lakes Brewing Company in 1991. He became brewmaster there a year later and remained until 2000, when he took a job as brewmaster at Frederick Brewing Company in Maryland; he followed that with a five-year stint as brewmaster at Dogfish Head.

McNulty had jumped on the opportunity to bring him back to Cleveland. "I was backpacking in Thailand, (and) I stopped in a bar in Bangkok that had Wi-Fi," he told Michael Heaton of the *Plain Dealer*. "I happened on a blog that said Andy was leaving Dogfish Head. I e-mailed my business partners right away and told them we have to get this guy. He does amazing things in the brewhouse."

The beer garden at Market Garden Brewery in Ohio City is a popular outdoor drinking spot in virtually all weather. *Photo by Leslie Basalla.*

Given Tveekrem's impressive brewing résumé and Dogfish Head's reputation for crafting unusual and off-the-wall beers ("Off-Centered Ales for Off-Centered People," as the brewery's slogan goes), local beer geeks had high expectations for Market Garden's beers and were somewhat confused and confounded to find that the brewery focused on sessionable and approachable beers in classic styles. Nevertheless, the brewery quickly became a popular destination and nightlife hotspot. The beer garden, in particular, was a draw, filling up in anything resembling decent weather with revelers eagerly downing glasses of Pearl Street Wheat, the brewery's popular hefeweizen, and Viking, its balanced pale ale.

"Standing on this patio you get the whole vibe of Ohio City," McNulty told the *Plain Dealer*'s John Petkovic. "It's a real urban neighborhood with a proud past that's coming back to life."

When it first opened, Market Garden was slated to feature a distillery in addition to the brewery. The intent was for the company to become the first making liquor in Cleveland since Prohibition. Another brewery/distillery, Portside, beat it to that milestone in 2012. It is not clear if those plans have been scuttled or are still in place but on indefinite hold because of the high level of traffic Market Garden receives and the company's other ventures.

Market Garden expanded its dining space within a year of opening, adding the Ohio City Room, a ninety-seat dining room and bar below ground level. Between its many spaces, the brewery hosts multiple special events, including private functions like wedding rehearsal dinners and corporate parties, and public events like the monthly literary reading series, Brew and Prose.

In a communal spirit, typical of McNulty's neighborhood booster-ism, Market Garden often collaborates with other area breweries and institutions. It brewed an Extra IPA called Market Centennial in honor of its neighbor the West Side Market's 100th anniversary in 2012 and worked with Great Lakes on a pair of special beers to celebrate the pioneering brewery's 25th anniversary in 2013. McNulty is quick to credit the Conways' brewery with laying the groundwork for his ventures in the area.

"I have a ton of respect for Pat and Dan," McNulty said. "They were on the cutting edge of urban redevelopment. They were the real risk-takers coming into the neighborhood."

There is also camaraderie between the two breweries, partially born as a result of Tveekrem's history with Great Lakes. "We don't view each other as competitors," McNulty said. "Andy hired [current Great Lakes brewmaster] Luke Purcell. Fast-forward all these years later, and he and Andy share ingredients."

Like its neighbor, Market Garden has expanded its beer menu over time, and several of the original recipes have evolved, with some getting a little bolder in terms of flavor and alcohol content. Part of that transition was aided and abetted by McNulty and company's next move.

Nano Brew Cleveland

Little more than a year after opening, Market Garden suddenly had a little sister brewery. Located a block north at the corner of West Twenty-fifth Street and Bridge Avenue, Nano Brew Cleveland opened in the summer of 2012 and, in addition to offering another beer-centric destination for the neighborhood, also offered Market Garden's brew team a place to experiment with new recipes. Many breweries have a small, "pilot" system for this purpose, but McNulty and his partners chose to build a bar around the concept.

An exterior shot of Nano Brew Cleveland in the Ohio City neighborhood. *Photo by Leslie Basalla.*

While Nano's flagship offerings, including Namber Amber Ale, are brewed on Market Garden's ten-barrel system, the bar features a small twenty-gallon brewhouse where Tveekrem's assistant brewers try out new ideas and offer them to the public. The ones that succeed make it into Nano's regular rotation, and Nano beers that do especially well "graduate" and become Market Garden beers. One of Market Garden's flagships, Citramax IPA, started out as a Nano brew, and a few others, including Particle Accelerator, an imperial rye IPA, and #Kolsch also recently migrated down the street.

Nano has a casual, neighborhood vibe. The bar features a bicycle theme, with vintage cycles and parts adorning the walls, and a converted shipping container "bike box" for parking outside. A giant Jenga set, made from foot-long sections of two-by-fours offers entertainment for guests.

Nano expanded its footprint in early 2015, after its former next-door neighbor, the French-inspired farm-to-table restaurant the Black Pig, moved a few blocks west. Now occupying three storefronts instead of one, Nano isn't so nano anymore. As the summer of 2015 got underway, the company's contractors were busy connecting the upper-level patio that the Black Pig left behind with Nano's outdoor bar and beer garden.

Some may question McNulty and company's business strategy of locating so many concepts in such a small geographic area, but McNulty insists it is working.

"They flourished," he said in a statement. "Each opening was different. And each brought more visitors to Cleveland's burgeoning beer district, demonstrating the truth in the urban planning ideal of having the highest amount of choice in the smallest amount of area."

THE BOTTLEHOUSE BREWERY

While McNulty was making a big splash on the west side with Market Garden, a couple Cleveland Heights residents were quietly creating a brewery that would come to be a hub of their east side neighborhood.

Brian Benchek and Dave Schubert were neighbors on the same block, their kids were about the same age and both men shared an interest in brewing. They regularly made the crosstown trek together to the Brew Kettle to make batches of beer in the brew-on-premise. Eventually, on one of those long, most-likely buzzed, trips back home, the two hit upon the idea of opening a brew-on-premise right in their own neighborhood. Neither had ever run a bar or restaurant before, but the two decided to give it a try.

"We thought, 'if we don't do this, someone else will," Schubert said in a *Cleveland Magazine* article.

The BottleHouse opened in May 2012, in a building that had previously housed Zagara's grocery store's cold storage. The space was lofty yet laid back, with wooden picnic tables, a cluster of pinball machines and a bookshelf loaded with board games. A large stage, complete with drums and a vintage electric organ, filled the west wall, and behind a small, steel-topped bar, veteran bartender and cocktail savant Tommy Mullady slung classic and original mixed drinks alongside the house beers. A massive conical sculpture of innumerable tubes of red, hand-blown glass was suspended from the ceiling. Benchek, an artist and glassblower, made and installed it himself. It was everything that Benchek and Schubert hoped it would be. "It's more like a coffeehouse," Schubert said. "Nothing scary or threatening. Nothing you wouldn't want to expose your young children to." On any day, seemingly half the guests in the brewery had walked there from the surrounding blocks, and many came with kids in tow.

Benchek and Schubert had installed ten half-barrel kettles and were ready to help Heights residents brew their own beer, but thanks to the bar's immediate popularity within its densely populated neighborhood, things didn't pan out exactly as the duo planned. It became clear, within just months of opening, that demand for the house beers was so high that they could afford neither the time nor the fermenter space to operate the brew-on-premise. By August, the BOP was indefinitely (and probably permanently) on the back burner.

"It's just a matter of demand for our beer," Benchek told the *Akron Beacon Journal*'s Rick Armon. "We're very happy with the quality of our beer. We're just trying to keep up with demand."

The problem then became how to make consistent, quality batches of beer on a system meant to make multiple, much-smaller batches and how to ferment it in equipment that was never meant for use in a commercial brewery. Utilizing every bit of scrappy, shoestring ingenuity at his disposal, Benchek managed to make it work, putting out a variety of styles including a fine Kolsch, several IPAs and an excellent coffee stout brewed in collaboration with Ohio City's Rising Star Roasters, until finally in late 2014, the brewery upgraded to a seven-barrel system, complete with proper, glycol-jacketed fermenters.

Just as Benchek was nimble enough to alter his business model when it became necessary and adapt the brewery's equipment to its changing needs, he also encouraged his employees' talents and allowed their ideas to shape the direction of the BottleHouse. When bartender Jason Kallicragas suggested the brewery try making mead (honey wine), Benchek gave him the time and supplies to experiment. The first batches of mead were a success. In early 2014, the brewery purchased a winery license, allowing it to make and sell meads at higher ABVs than its beer, and mead now shares equal billing with beer among its offerings. At most times, there are six to eight of each available on tap, making the BottleHouse both a brewery and the Cleveland area's first commercial meadery. Kallicragas remains the head mead-maker, as well as taproom manager and assistant brewer.

With the new brewing equipment in place, the BottleHouse plans to distribute beer and possibly mead in a limited area, primarily around Cleveland Heights. Mostly, however, the owners are content to keep their role as a home-away-from-home for their neighborhood.

"Every brewery can't be Sierra Nevada–size or Sam Adams," Kallicragas said. "But every neighborhood can have a brewery this size."

OTHER BREWERIES: 2006–2010

One could easily be misled, given the hype around Fat Heads and the emerging Ohio City brewer's row, to believe that no one else in the Cleveland area opened a brewery in the late 2000s. A look to the outer fringes of the region proves that notion wrong. To the east, in Lake and Geauga Counties, the Main Street Grille in Garrettsville opened in 2007, followed by Cellar Rats, in the Debonne Winery complex, in 2008 and in 2010, Chardon Brew Works and Little Mountain Brewing Company (which opened first in Kirtland and later relocated to Mentor). The year 2010 also saw the opening of the brewing arm of Lager Heads Smoke House in Medina. Akron welcomed Hoppin' Frog in 2006. Hoppin' Frog has consistently been voted one of the best breweries in the world by RateBeer.com users, thanks largely to brewmaster/owner Fred Karm's geek-friendly, high-powered, often barrel-aged stouts and other small-batch rarities.

OHIO CITY BREWS BIGGER

Back in Ohio City, Sam McNulty's grander ambitions are on their way to being fulfilled. While Market Garden's capacity has held steady at around two thousand barrels a year since opening, it will not remain there for long. Unlike many other local brewers, McNulty and his partners have steadfastly (some would say stubbornly) refused to get into packaging and distribution. Market Garden beer is available only on the premises and at its sister bars on West Twenty-fifth Street, but a production brewery in the works will change that. Expected to open in late 2015 and affectionately dubbed the "Palace of Fermentation," Market Garden's production works will have a starting capacity of twenty-five thousand barrels but should reach seventy-five thousand once fully built out. The facility will allow Market Garden beer to be distributed across the Cleveland area and eventually all over Ohio. Another start-up brewery in the Ohio City neighborhood, however, is already proving that a big production plant isn't necessary for getting its product into bars and stores all over Cleveland.

The Market Garden Brewery brewhouse building was once a poultry slaughterhouse, and old hand-painted images on the building depict chickens and ducks. *Photo by Leslie Basalla.*

Chapter 13
THE RISING TIDE

NEW BREWERIES FLOOD THE CITY

In 2013, word hit the local media that another new brewery was coming to Ohio City. One might have expected the owners of the area's established breweries to greet the news with concern about increased competition, but instead, reaction was quite the opposite. When questioned, everyone with a stake in the neighborhood's beer business echoed the same mantra: "the rising tide lifts all ships."

"The fact that we can support so many new breweries as a city says something about the people of Cleveland—they love beer, and they love supporting their own," said Marissa DeSantis, public relations supervisor for Great Lakes.

Put another way by Sam McNulty, whose stated goal is for Ohio City to return to its historic role as the city's brewing hub, "We always welcome more craft brewers to enter the local market, especially if they want to join us in the Ohio City brewery district!"

It was fitting, then, that the first beer tapped at the new Platform Beer Company was a Belgian IPA, brewed in collaboration with Market Garden and called Rising Tides.

PLATFORM BEER COMPANY

Paul Benner opened the Cleveland Brew Shop, a homebrewing supply store, in Cleveland's Tremont neighborhood in 2012 and almost immediately noticed that his customers were all saying the same thing, usually something along the lines of, "I love brewing so much; I wish I could do this as a job instead of as just a hobby."

That got Benner thinking—a good craftsperson pursuing another pastime, like woodworking or jewelry making, could easily build a business by selling their handiwork, but because of legal restrictions, good homebrewers are not afforded the same opportunity. He wondered if there was a way he could create a legal "springboard" that would allow ambitious homebrewers an entrée into the world of professional brewing. A chance meeting with another young business owner, Justin Carson, who was looking to relocate his draft system installation and maintenance company, JC Beertech, led to the idea of Platform Beer Company, Cleveland's first and only incubator brewery.

The duo drafted brewmaster Shaun Yasaki, barely twenty-seven years old, who had made the leap from homebrewing to a commercial brewhouse thanks to Fat Heads' Matt Cole, who three years before had offered him an apprenticeship. The three went to work on converting a 100-plus-year-old Hungarian social club on the still-gentrifying western fringes of Ohio City into a new brewery and a new business model.

"It's not just another brewery," Benner said in a *Plain Dealer* interview. "The last thing I want is for a project I'm associated with to be viewed as just another opportunity to take advantage of a trend."

Opened in July 2014, Platform represented a different approach to the concept of a craft brewery in Cleveland. First there was the brewery incubator—Platform offers homebrewers who are considering going pro the opportunity to apply for an internship program in the brewery. Over twelve weeks, the incubator brewer works with Yasaki to learn the ins and outs of commercial brewing, including all the details of proper sanitation and equipment maintenance. He or she also receives guidance on scaling up recipes to a commercial size and gets to have two beers featured on draft in Platform's taproom. At the same time, the participant also pairs with Benner and Carson to receive a crash course in the entrepreneurial skills needed to launch a new beer business, including how to court investors, source buildings and equipment, write a business plan and navigate liquor laws and even some basics in advertising and marketing. If all goes correctly, a graduate of the incubator program will come out armed with all the skills he or she needs to start a new brewery.

Beyond the incubator, though, Platform separated itself by eschewing both the brewpub model and that of the production-only brewery. Benner calls the brewery's atmosphere a "West Coast–vibe tasting room."

Instead of housing the brew kettles and fermenters behind glass, only the bar and some hip-high half-walls separate patrons from the sounds and smells of whatever Yasaki is doing in the brewhouse. There is no kitchen—Platform instead partners with a rotating cast of area restaurants, culinary start-ups and food trucks to provide meals for patrons during peak hours. There is no table service; everyone orders drinks at the bar, and a self-serve water station parked between the vintage bowling machine and the food counter allows guests to hydrate themselves at will.

Although it initially confused some guests who were accustomed to the full-service, full-bar brewpub model that has largely become the standard in Cleveland, Platform's casual, beer-centric approach was quickly embraced, and the brewery grew within its first year into an anchor for the emerging stretch of Lorain Avenue it occupied.

It also didn't take long for Platform to grow in capacity. The brewery opened with a 3.5-barrel brew system, which was mostly intended for use by the incubator and for experimental beers. A 10-barrel system was already on order from custom fabricator Portland Kettle Works but took nearly five more months to arrive and another month to install. Once the new system was in place, along with several additional fermenters and brite tanks sourced from a defunct area brewery, Platform's capacity tripled. The brewery expects to reach 2,500 barrels of output in its first full year in business and has already started distributing kegs to area bars and restaurants and canning its first flagship beer, New Cleveland, a "palesner" brewed with pilsner malts and Noble German hops but an ale yeast. A second canned beer, Speed Merchant White IPA, saw local distribution by midsummer of 2015.

Not quite content with Platform's initial success, Benner and Carson have already expanded their horizons. The two bought one of the last remaining buildings of the old Leisy Brewing Company complex in early 2015 and plan to have it up and running as Gypsy Brewery by the end of the year. The brewery will serve as Platform's production arm, as well as a contract brewing facility for other small brewers who are looking to move into distribution but lack the space and capacity to do so. The building will also feature one level devoted to raw, open event space.

Platform was far from the only brewery to arrive on the Cleveland scene in 2014, though. The months following its July opening would be some of the most eventful in Cleveland brewing history.

HISTORY & REVIVAL IN THE RUST BELT

BUTCHER AND THE BREWER

Hot on Platform's heels came another highly anticipated development on both Cleveland's restaurant and craft beer scene. In August 2014, the long-awaited Butcher and the Brewer opened in downtown Cleveland's burgeoning East Fourth Street entertainment district. Sharing a block with the likes of celebrity chef Michael Symon's Lola Bistro and Cleveland's House of Blues franchise, Butcher was in good company but up against stiff competition. Owned by Chris Lieb, whose Tremont Taphouse gastropub has been a fixture on the local craft beer scene since 2005, Butcher and the Brewer is a high-concept operation that encompasses an upscale restaurant and brewpub on one side and is slated to house an artisanal butcher and charcuterie shop on the other.

The timing of the opening could not have been better. Downtown Cleveland was in the midst of a residential renaissance, with apartment occupancy north of 95 percent, even as developers scrambled to convert more and more moribund office blocks into residential units. On top of that, a new casino had opened, prodigal son LeBron James had announced his impending return to the Cleveland Cavaliers and the city had just completed a new Medical Mart and Convention Center only blocks away. Under those auspicious conditions, Lieb and company unveiled their ambitious new brewery.

Visually, Butcher and the Brewer is a marvel. Housed in a former department store but stripped to the bones for an industrial-chic vibe, it boasts towering whitewashed concrete ceilings and pillars, custom-made reclaimed wood and steel furniture, a chalkboard mural depicting the brewing process and, at the back, a gleaming, ten-barrel brewhouse set into a subway-tiled alcove.

The brewer behind Butcher and the Brewer is Eric Anderson, an alumnus of Buckeye Brewing, with a degree in microbiology. In the short time that Butcher and the Brewer has been open, Anderson has shown a capricious disregard for the established boundaries of beer styles, brewing concoctions like an "Albino Stout" (pale gold in color but exhibiting all of the chocolate and coffee characteristics of a regular, black stout) and an imperial hoppy hefeweizen, alongside more conventional offerings like saisons and IPAs. It remains to be seen if his mad scientist approach to brewing will yield beer varieties that will catch on outside of his state-of-the-art brewhouse. Butcher and the Brewer will eventually distribute beers under the name the Cleveland Brewing Company.

CLEVELAND BEER

BRICK AND BARREL

Irishtown Bend in Cleveland's Flats, although located right around the corner from Ohio City and only a twist of the river away from the old Flats entertainment district, has always been a quiet, mixed-use neighborhood, with houses and condos lining the Columbus Avenue hill and the venerable old dive bar Major Hooples as its anchor. Across the iconic, green lift bridge sit warehouses, a pizzeria and bar, a small park and the docks and storage facility from which the Cleveland Rowing Foundation launches its sculls.

Things started changing in the summer of 2014, when Cleveland Metroparks opened Rivergate Park and a new restaurant, Merwin's Wharf, next to the rowing foundation, and the city of Cleveland relocated its skate park into the same area. The bend was becoming something of an outdoor recreation complex. It was into this eclectic milieu that peripatetic winemaker and brewer Karl Spiesman located his Brick and Barrel brewery in late 2014.

In 2003, after spending five years in the Coast Guard, the Lake County native took a job as a "cellar rat" at Debonne Vineyards. "You do everything," he told the *Plain Dealer*'s Marc Bona. "Tanks, sanitation, you do maintenance on the pumps, you learn how to fix things. You take your mechanical inclination to a new level. I was a wine janitor."

It was enough to get Spiesman interested in the art of fermentation—it wasn't enough to satisfy his wanderlust, though, and for the next decade he made an itinerant living, bouncing from winery to brewery and back, on both coasts of the United States and at least one other continent. His résumé includes stints at vineyards in Sonoma, California; Oregon's Willamette Valley; and Hawkes Bay, New Zealand. He put in time at Harpoon Brewery in Vermont, where he started again in the cellars but worked his way up to the brewhouse, and at Full Sail in Oregon. He made his way back to Ohio in 2010, put down roots, got married and started to think about opening his own brewery and winery.

Joined by partners Mike Dagiasis and Jason Henkel, he began construction on Brick and Barrel in January 2014, with doors opening almost a year later in December. Brick and Barrel is a true nanobrewery, with Spiesman brewing on a three-and-a-half-barrel system. Like Platform, it is a casual taproom, with the brewing apparatus separated from the bar area by little more than a reclaimed steel work table. There is no kitchen, but Merwin's Wharf and next-door neighbors the Rivergate Tavern and Sainato's Pizza will deliver food to patrons.

A glass garage door opens on to a small street patio in warm weather, and Spiesman has plans to open a back patio, with a view of the overhead RTA Rapid Transit trestle. The interior is as eclectic as Spiesman's résumé—the bar is constructed from old church pews and topped with chalkboard reclaimed from a renovation at Lakewood High School. Gymnasium floor from the high school, with basketball court lines still intact, makes up several tabletops. Spiesman's wife, Elina, curates an ever-changing display of original paintings and sculpture by local artists.

The brewery typically features four to six of its own beers at any given time, including some higher-powered options like McTavish, a rich, malty Scotch Wee Heavy. While the addition of a new fermenter will increase Brick and Barrel's capacity slightly, Spiesman doesn't look to expand brewing operations much beyond that. What really has him excited is the addition of wine making by the fall of 2015. He plans to source grapes from the Pacific Northwest and Long Island and offer barrel-sharing programs and private label wines for local restaurants.

Spiesman is optimistic about the growth of the craft brewing community in Cleveland.

"We are young and have a great craft brewing community that supports each other and looks not at competition but at collaborating together."

PORTSIDE BREWERY AND DISTILLERY

Technically, Portside Brewery and Distillery opened back in 2012, but it wasn't until January 2015 that the brewing and rum-making concern was able to open a permanent tasting room. Helmed by former Great Lakes chemist, Dan Malz, the company launched its rums and began brewing beer a few months later in April 2013.

Located on Front Street at the northernmost end of West Ninth Street and facing out toward the Port of Cleveland and Browns Stadium, Portside straddles the boundary between the Warehouse District and the redeveloping East Bank of the Flats and is the first commercial distillery in the city of Cleveland since Prohibition. It offers five varieties of rum—silver, hopped, spiced, maple-vanilla and a Christmas rum with spices.

The tasting room, carved into the ground level of the Port Authority offices, features exposed brick and sandstone and offers guests views into the brewhouse and the distillery. A barn door separates a private dining/party room, and a small menu of snacks prepped by neighboring restaurant the Willeyville is available.

Portside's beers were available on local shelves before the tasting room ever opened. The company partnered with local TV comedy icon Big Chuck Schodowski to launch a canned 11.7 percent barleywine in 2014. Beers on tap in the tasting room have names that reference shipping and seafaring, such as the Ironclad IPA and Bismarck Baltic Porter, but the flagship, also available in bottled six-packs, is 216 Pale Ale, a proud shout-out to Cleveland's area code.

In addition to so many small, local breweries, 2014 also saw the arrival of international brewery chain and beer hall HofbrauHaus in Cleveland's Playhouse Square district.

ESTABLISHED AND EXPANDING

Not to be outdone or overshadowed by the influx of new brewers on the Cleveland scene, many of the city's older, better established breweries have recently taken advantage of the area's mounting interest in and insatiable thirst for craft beer to expand their footprints, both physically and distribution-wise.

Great Lakes Brewing Company unveiled new visual branding in 2015, the first time its packaging, tap handles and logos have been updated in the brewery's nearly thirty-year history. As part of its new look, the brewery also opened a visitor's center called the Beer Symposium with rotating exhibits and artifacts from its storied past.

Several new seasonal offerings, including Lawn Seat Kolsch and High Striker Belgian Single, arrived in a mixed twelve-pack in the spring of 2015, and the brewery introduced a wheat session IPA, called Sharpshooter—named in tribute to Ohio native Annie Oakley. Great Lakes also maxed out its brewing capacity over 2014 and 2015, first moving its offices out of the brewing facility to make room for two six-hundred-barrel brite tanks and four six-hundred-barrel fermenters and then added a seventy-five-barrel fermenter for smaller batch selections. The brewery ranked, at the end of 2014, as the twenty-third-largest craft brewer in the nation, according to the Brewer's Association.

The Brew Kettle, which is already expected to brew at least ten thousand barrels this year, announced plans in February 2015 that it would open a second location in the Lorain County suburb of Amherst, Ohio. Owner Chris Russo is an Amherst native and recognized that the area was underserved both for craft beer and quality restaurants. There were no plans, as of this printing, to include a brew-on-premise in the new location. The company also oversaw passage of legislation in Strongsville that will allow it to combine its production and retail operations into a single, new facility sometime in the future.

The Brew Kettle also utilized its increased brewing capacity to begin packaging and distributing additional beers. Its popular Kitka Milk Stout recently appeared in bottles alongside the brewery's flagships, and the brewery debuted its first canned beer, Awesome India Pale Lager. The brewery also partnered with the red-hot Cleveland Cavaliers to market a session India Pale Ale called All for One, which is available at the Quicken Loans Arena, as well as at retail outlets and the brewpub. In collaboration with Cedar Point amusement park, a Munich-style lager called Rougabrew arrived just in time for the park to debut its newest roller coaster, the Rougarou.

Buckeye Brewing opened a taproom in its Walford Avenue production facility in early 2015. Named TapStack, in reference to the building's towering smokestack, which can be seen for miles around, the quirky space dispenses both tried-and-true Buckeye classics, like Cleveland IPA and Christmas Girl, alongside new, experimental concoctions. Its location right next door to Ray's Indoor Mountain Bike park ensures a steady clientele of thirsty riders.

Fat Heads continued to expand in 2014 and 2015, adding ten new 120-barrel fermenters to its production brewery in Middleburg Heights. The increased tank space allowed the brewery to hit 20,000 barrels in 2014, with production expected to top 35,000 barrels in 2015. The brewery plans to expand into an adjoining warehouse over the following year, increasing capacity as it goes. As the plant's capacity has grown, Fat Heads packaged offerings have also diversified. In additional to bottling year-round flagships Bumbleberry, Head Hunter and Sunshine Daydream, the brewery started to bottle a number of seasonal and limited release beers, including its spiced Christmas ale, Holly Jolly; Bone Head Imperial Red; and Shakedown Stout.

In perhaps the most ambitious move a local brewery has ever undertaken, Fat Heads also opened a West Coast outpost in late 2014, planting a brewpub in Portland Oregon's Pearl District and thereby boldly staking a claim in the heart of the biggest craft brewing city in the nation.

SPINNING OFF:
THE BREWERY SCENE SPAWNS NEW BUSINESSES

In addition to slaking the thirsts of beer lovers, reviving neighborhoods and employing hundreds of people within the Cleveland area, local breweries have also enabled the development of a number of auxiliary and ancillary businesses.

In recent years, a number of brewery tour operators, including the Cleveland Brew Bus and Arlo's Craft Beer Guide, have been shuttling passengers to and from area breweries for guided tastings, beer education and brewhouse tours. Brewnuts, a Tremont culinary start-up, makes yeast-raised doughnuts that feature local craft beers in their ingredients.

Another business, Buckeye Canning, is affording small, up-and-coming breweries and rising stars like Fat Heads alike the opportunity to get more beer into the region's retail coolers. Literally a mobile canning operation, Buckeye Canning brings its equipment to breweries by truck and cans batches of beer on location, allowing smaller breweries the ability to distribute their products without investing in an expensive and space-consuming bottling line. In August 2015, Buckeye Canning announced that it would partner with eight Ohio breweries, including Cornerstone, Platform, Portside and Willoughby to provide canned craft beer for Cleveland Browns Stadium.

The growing popularity of homebrewing as a hobby has allowed supply stores, like Benner's Cleveland Brew Shop to expand. He recently relocated the brew shop to a much-larger storefront across the street from Platform. Homebrew clubs like the SNOBs and Society of Akron-Area Zymurgists (SAAZ) have also seen increases in membership and enjoy the support of many local breweries, which happily host their events and meetings.

Hop farming is taking hold in Ohio's agricultural heartland and in Cleveland's many urban farms and community gardens. Although very little infrastructure for processing hops yet exists, the bitter cones seem poised to become another cash crop in the Buckeye State. Great Lakes sources hops locally from its neighbor, the Ohio City Farm, and from its own Pint Size Farm located in the Cuyahoga Valley National Park's historic Hale Farm and Village.

As interest in craft beer has increased in the area, many local restaurants and bars have made it a focal point of their offerings. Alongside classic gastropubs like Tremont Taphouse and Buckeye Beer Engine and pioneering pub chain the Winking Lizard, whose World Beer Tour program has opened many local minds and palates, restaurants like Demetrios Atheneos's Oak

Barrel and Forage Public House, Deagan's Kitchen and Bar, Alan Glazen's ABC and XYZ Taverns, Barrio Tacos, City Tap and the Melt Bar and Grilled sandwich chain tout their broad-ranging draft selections of local, regional and national craft brews. The metro area also abounds with far too many quality beer stores to name, many of which offer growler-filling stations or even small bars at which patrons may purchase a beer to sip while perusing the merchandise. Many also offer beer-tasting events.

Cleveland Beer Week, the city's annual festival of all things craft beer was first celebrated in 2009 and has expanded every year since. It features hundreds of tastings, tap takeovers, beer pairings and other sudsy events in dozens of venues around town and culminates with a grand tasting, showcasing scores of breweries, called Brewzilla.

Bright Horizons: Even More Breweries in the Works

The growth of the Cleveland beer scene, if anything, is accelerating rather than slowing down. If 2014 and early 2015 saw a groundswell of breweries within the boundaries of Cleveland proper, the ensuing year promises more of the same.

In April, the Cleveland Brewery, which had been quietly supplying beers to restaurants in its North Collinwood neighborhood, finally opened the doors to its East 185th Street tasting room.

Developer Rick Semersky has ambitious plans to transform the neighborhood around his historic Slovenian restaurant, Sterle's Country House on East Fifty-fifth Street. Anchoring his multi-pronged build out will be Hub 55, a mixed-use retail/restaurant complex that will house a breakfast and lunch café; an incubator market for craftspeople, culinary start-ups and local farmers; and Goldhorn Brewery. Former Great Lakes pub brewer Joel Warger was expected to start churning out Goldhorn's Central European–inspired brews by October. Semersky has also partnered with the first graduate of Platform Beer Company's incubator program, Kyle Roth, to launch Ferndock Brewing in Sandusky.

Another brewery with Slovenian roots should finally open its doors, right around the corner from Market Garden and Great Lakes, sometime this year. The Hansa Brewery, located in a revamped and expanded version of Boris Music's European grocery store and travel agency, the Hansa Import

House, has been under construction for two years but appears to be nearing completion. Hansa will feature recipes from Slovenian brewery Lasko.

Also around the corner from Ohio City and just up the hill from Brick and Barrel, Forest City Brewery (the fourth to operate under that name in Cleveland) is expected to be open in the Duck Island neighborhood by fall. Forest City's building dates back to the 1860s and once housed a German-owned saloon. The building will be something of a craft beverage hub—it is also slated to include the Western Reserve Meadery and Duck-Rabbit Coffee Roasters.

Plans are also in the works for Birdtown Brewery, which will take over a decommissioned church in Lakewood's historic, working-class Birdtown neighborhood. Local media also reported on Kennedy Craft Beer, which received permitting from the city of Westlake in early 2015.

There appears to be no end in sight for Cleveland's current craft beer boom. As the scene has grown, it has attracted national media attention. *Conde Nast Traveler* named Cleveland one of America's best beer cities in a January 2015 issue, and similar accolades appeared on websites including the Thrillist and the Huffington Post. That good press coincided with a number of publications from the *New York Times* to *Travel and Leisure* naming Cleveland a top travel destination for 2015.

Platform's Shaun Yasaki is optimistic for Cleveland's craft beer future. "Cleveland has a young beer scene," he said. "People are still learning about craft beer. [There's] plenty of room for growth—probably at the expense of large, national craft breweries, but that's OK."

Sam McNulty, characteristically, has even higher hopes. "Give us three years," he told *Edible Cleveland*. "We'll be the number one destination for craft beer in the world. Yes, I said 'world.'"

BIBLIOGRAPHY

Books, Magazines and Journals

Armon, Rick. "Exploring the Cleveland Beer Scene." *All About Beer Magazine*, June 2014.

———. *Ohio Breweries*. Mechanicsburg, PA: Stackpole Books, 2011.

Blessing, Anna H. *Locally Brewed: Portraits of Craft Breweries from America's Heartland*. Chicago, IL: Agate Midway Publishers, 2014.

Brill, Jason. "Bottle Service: Brian Bencheck and Dave Schubert Offer East Side Beer Fans a Brew-It-Yourself Spot." *Cleveland Magazine*, July 2012.

———. "Brew Crew." *Cleveland Magazine*, October 2014.

Butler, Margaret Manor. *A Pictorial History of the Western Reserve, 1796–1860*. Cleveland, OH: Western Reserve Historical Society, Lakewood Historical Society, 1963.

Callahan, Nelson J., and William F. Hickey. *Irish Americans and Their Communities of Cleveland*. Cleveland, OH: Cleveland State University Press, 1978.

Carr, Kathy Ames. "The Rising Tide of Local Craft Breweries." *Edible Cleveland*, Fall 2014.

Gerlat, Allen. "Unconventional Brewery Pours Over Strategies. Brothers Push Sustainability in Cleveland." *Waste News*, February 19, 2007.

Glanville, Justin. "Cleveland's Rich Beer History: Pat Conway Tells All." *Edible Cleveland*, Fall 2014.

BIBLIOGRAPHY

Hieronymus, Stan. "The Class of '88: Looking Back at a Quarter Century of Business, Beer and People." *All About Beer Magazine* 34, no. 6 (January 2014).

Hitch, John. "Brew Love: Sam McNulty Believes in Beer." *Cleveland Magazine*, September 2011.

Miller, Carl H. *Breweries of Cleveland*. Cleveland, OH: Schnitzelbank Press, 1998.

Mittleman, Amy. *Brewing Battles: A History of American Beer*. New York: Algora Publishing, 2007.

Mosher, Randy. *Tasting Beer: An Insider's Guide to the World's Greatest Drink*. North Adams, MA: Storey Publishing, 2009.

Musson, Robert A., MD. *Brewing Beer in the Buckeye State, Volume 1: A History of the Brewing Industry in Eastern Ohio from 1808 to 2004*. Medina, OH: Zepp Publications, 2005.

———. *Brewing in Cleveland*. Mount Pleasant, SC: Arcadia Publishing, 2005.

Oliver, Garrett. *The Oxford Companion to Beer*. New York: Oxford University Press, Inc., 2012.

Rice, Harvey. *Sketches of Western Reserve Life*. Cleveland, OH: William W. Williams, 1885.

Rich, H.S., and Co. *One Hundred Years of Brewing: A Complete History of the Progress Made in the Art, Science and Industry of Brewing in the World, Particularly in the Last Century*. Chicago, IL: H.S. Rich & Co., 1903.

Richmond, Lesley, and Alison Turto. *The Brewing Industry: A Guide to Historical Records*. Manchester, UK: Manchester University Press, 1990.

Rose, William Ganson. *Cleveland: The Making of a City*. Cleveland, OH: World Publishing Company. 1950.

Van Tassel, David D., and John J. Grabowski. *The Dictionary of Cleveland Biography*. Bloomington: Indiana University Press (in conjunction with Case Western Reserve University and the Western Reserve Historical Society), 1996.

———. *The Encyclopedia of Cleveland History*. Bloomington: Indiana University Press (in conjunction with Case Western Reserve University and the Western Reserve Historical Society), 1996.

Wheeler, Robert A. *Visions of the Western Reserve: Public and Private Documents of Northeastern Ohio, 1750–1860*. Columbus: The Ohio State University Press, 2000.

Whittlesey, Colonel Charles. *Early History of Cleveland, Ohio*. Cleveland, OH: Fairbanks, Benedict and Co., 1867.

BIBLIOGRAPHY

Interviews and Personal Discussions

Benner, Paul. Owner, Platform Beer Company. April 2015.

DeSantis, Marissa. Public relations supervisor, Great Lakes Brewing Company. April 2015.

Kallicragas, Jason. Assistant brewerm/taproom manager/mead maker, the Bottlehouse Brewery. April 2015.

McNulty, Sam. Owner, Market Garden Brewery and Nano Brew Cleveland. April 2015

Spiesman, Karl. Owner/brewmaster, Brick and Barrel. April 2015.

Tveekrem, Andy. Brewmaster/owning partner, Market Garden Brewery and Nano Brew Cleveland. April 2015.

Warger, Joel. Brewmaster, Goldhorn Brewery. April 2015.

Welliver, Jerome. Owner, Black Box Brewing Company and J.W. Dover. April 2015.

Yasaki, Shaun. Brewmaster, Platform Beer Company. April 2015.

Newspaper Articles

Akron Beacon Journal. "Great Lakes Celebrates 25 Years of Great Beer. 'Heritage Brewer' Helps Shape Industry and Transform Cleveland Neighborhood." September 4, 2013.

———. "Market Garden, Great Lakes Are Working Together. Breweries Collaborating to Produce Three Beers for Ohio City Neighborhood Event on May 10." May 1, 2013.

Cleveland (OH) Plain Dealer. "Award-Winning Brewer to Open Local Fat Heads." January 7, 2009.

———. "Beer's 'Patron Saint' May Soon Rule Over Market Square Park. McNulty, Others Aim to Restore Statue." December 10, 2014.

———. "Cleveland Heights' BottleHouse Is a Beer Joint Where You BYO Food." June 8, 2012.

———. "Drink a Toast to This: Ohio City to Get Another Brewery, Eatery. Hansa House to Become Complex Serving European Cuisine, Slovenian Beer." April 26, 2013.

———. "Entrepreneurs Envision Brewery Incubator in Ohio City, Where Medina Company Is Moving Its Offices." July 24, 2013.

———. "Getting into a Froth: Willoughby Brew Pub Installs Its Equipment." November 19, 1997.

BIBLIOGRAPHY

———. "Great Lakes Brewing Co. Trivia—16 Facts You Might Not Know." September 13, 2013.

———. "Great Lakes Brewing Is 25, but Near-West Side Institution's Beginning in 1988 Was Risky." September 6, 2013.

———. "Karl Spiesman Has Had Many Wine, Beer Jobs—Even 'Cellar Rat.'" April 15, 2015.

———. "Leisy Brewing Co. Building Will See Beer Flow Again, Under Ohio City Contract-Brewing Plan. March 29, 2015.

———. "Make Beer, Friends at the Brew Kettle. Staff Helps Customers Through the Process." January 7, 2015.

———. "Matt Cole of Fat Head's Brewery in North Olmsted Heads to England for Special Brewing Collaboration." August 27, 2011.

———. "Micro to Macro: Brewers Expand, Brothers Say Their Latest Efforts Will Push Growing Great Lakes Brewery to a Fresh, Tasty New Level." October 29, 1999.

———. "Much-Anticipated Hub 55 Project in Cleveland's St. Clair-Superior Neighborhood Reveals Plans for Brewery." November 3, 2014.

———. "'Nano' Business Is Step Toward Brewery District." April 12, 2012.

———. "Noted Brewmaster Returns to Cleveland to Pour Energies Into New Microbrewery." January 12, 2010.

———. "On the Job: Chuck Gets a Taste of the Hard Work of Brewing Beer." November 27, 2009.

———. "Party Like Its 1999 BC? The Bottlehouse in Cleveland Heights Has Some Mead for You." June 13, 2014.

———. "Patrick Conway, the Man Behind Great Lakes Brewing and Christmas Ale." July 18, 2011.

———. "Portside Brewery, Buckeye Canning Systems to Can Craft Beer; Release Set for February." January 15, 2014.

———. "Portside Distillery and Brewery Plans Grand Opening." January 5, 2015.

———. "Sam McNulty's Market Garden Brewery and Distillery Embraces, Enhances Ohio City." June 29, 2011.

———. "Tapping Into City's History: Former Tavern to House Brewery." November 16, 2014.

———. "Trail Head Pale Ale from Fat Head's Brewery Raises Money for Cleveland Metroparks Trails Fund, Just in Time for National Trails Day." June 3, 2014.

Cleveland Scene. "Buckeye Brewing to Join the Taproom Revolution." March 3, 2014.

BIBLIOGRAPHY

———. "Canned History: The Revival of Locally Canned Beer." September 18, 2013.

———. "Get to Know Your Local Brewer." July 31, 2013.

———. "Liquid Gold: Bottlehouse Brewery in Cleveland Heights Is the City's First Full-Fledged Meadery, but the Brewers Say There's Room for Competition." July 2, 2014.

———. "Market Garden Brewery Orders Brewhouse Equipment for 'Palace of Fermentation.'" March 13, 2014.

———. "More on Tap: Think Cleveland Has a Lot of Breweries? Just Wait, More Will Be Opening Their Doors This Year." March 12, 2014.

———. "Nano Brew to Double in Size, but Will Remain Small at Heart). November 11, 2014.

Cleveland Scene. "New Brewery Brick and Barrel on Tap for the Flats." April 29, 2014.

———. "The Brew Kettle Will Open a Second Location in Amherst." February 27, 2015.

———. "The Daring Butcher and the Brewer Makes Its Mark on East Fourth." November 19, 2014.

———. "The Heart of It All: Fat Heads Launches Taproom in Brewery Production Facility." May 22, 2013.

———. "The King of the Taps: Shaun Yasaki." July 9, 2014.

———. "Two Breweries Expand, Two New Taprooms Open." December 16, 2014.

———. "Very Big Things Brewing for Brew Kettle." March 4, 2013.

Crain's Cleveland Business. "Growth on Tap at Great Lakes. Ohio City Brewer Creates Buzz With $6 Million in Capital Improvements That Will Bolster Production." September 27, 2010.

———. "Ohio City Brewer Is Building Quite a Platform." May 17, 2015.

———. "Overflowing with Optimism: Local Craft Brewers Are Expanding Operations to Keep Up With Increased Production." October 6, 2014.

Middleburg Heights (OH) Sun News. "Fat Heads in Middleburg Heights to Open Tasting Room." February 16, 2013.

Pittsburgh (PA) Post-Gazette. "Fat Heads Expanding to Cleveland Suburb, Where It Will Brew." August 21, 2008.

Strongsville (OH) Sun News. "Shake up at The Brew Kettle Could Result in Expansion Beyond Strongsville." March 28, 2013.

———. "With Demand Growing, Brew Kettle Expands Strongsville Brewery." August 28, 2012.

BIBLIOGRAPHY

Willoughby (OH) News-Herald. "Willoughby Brewing Co.'s Ownership Change Will Offer a Blend of New Ideas and Upholding Previous Ones." January 21, 2011.

Websites

American Breweriana Association. http://www.americanbreweriana.org (accessed on April 24, 2015).

The Artful Pint—Ohio Craft Beer—Born and Brewed. http://artfulpint. com (accessed on May 17, 2015).

The Beer Blog—Ohio. http://www.ohio.com/blogs/the-beer-blog (accessed on May 19, 2015).

Beer Books. http://www.beerbooks.com/ (accessed on April 28, 2015).

Brewers Association. https://www.brewersassociation.org (accessed on May 11, 2015).

Brewer's Daughter. http://www.brewersdaughter.com (accessed on May 24, 2015).

Claire Gebben Blog on Cleveland Brewing. http://clairegebben. com/2013/05/16/brewing-in-cleveland (accessed on May 24, 2015).

Cleveland Historical. http://clevelandhistorical.org (accessed on February 20, 2015).

Cleveland Magazine: Your Guide to the Best of Cleveland, 2008. http:// www.clevelandmagazine.com/ME2/dirmod.asp?sid=E73ABD6180B4 4874871A91F6BA5C249C&nm=Arts+%26+Entertainment&type=Pu blishing&mod=Publications%3A%3AArticle&mid=1578600D8080459 6A222593669321019&tier=4&id=F18E6E80BC9D48518F590125F356 37DD (accessed on May 18, 2015).

Cleveland Memory Project: Cleveland Breweries. http://clevelandmemory. org/breweries/index.html (accessed on May 24, 2015).

CWRU Encyclopedia of Cleveland History Online: Brewing and Distilling History. http://ech.cwru.edu/ech-cgi/article.pl?id=BADI (accessed on May 24, 2015).

Digital History: Prohibition. http://www.digitalhistory.uh.edu/disp_ textbook.cfm?smtID=2&psid=3383 (accessed on May 24, 2015).

Great American Beer Festival, GABF Winners. https://www. greatamericanbeerfestival.com/the-competition/winners (accessed on May 20, 2015).

BIBLIOGRAPHY

Great Lakes Brewing Company: A Company History. https://www. greatlakesbrewing.com/company/history (accessed on May 19, 2015).

"Hey Mabel, Black Label" blog. The History of Carling Black Label Beer in the U.S.A. http://corzman2001.wix.com/heymabelblacklabel/id23.htm (accessed on May 24, 2015).

Lakeview Cemetery. Historical Spotlight: Cleveland's Brewing Heritage. http://www.lakeviewcemetery.com/newsletter-2014-fall-1.php (accessed on May 24, 2015).

Ohio Breweriana. http://www.ohiobreweriana.com (accessed on April 24, 2014).

PearedCreation.com. "Quick Facts on Standard Brewing Company." http://www.pearedcreation.com/ohio-brewery-history/cleveland-oh/ standard-brewing-company (accessed on May 24, 2015).

Westerville Library: The Anti-Saloon League. http://www.westervillelibrary. org/AntiSaloon (accessed on May 24, 2015).

Westerville Library: The Anti-Saloon League—A Growing Influence. http://www.westervillelibrary.org/antisaloon-growing-influence (accessed on May 24, 2015).

World Beer Cup. http://www.worldbeercup.org (accessed on May 20, 2015).

Newspapers and Magazines in Electronic Format

Bryan Times. "[Erin] Brew Is Returning." May 18, 1988, p11. Accessed via Google Reader https://news.google.com/newspapers?nid=799&dat=19 880518&id=LZFPAAAAIBAJ&sjid=o1EDAAAAIBAJ&pg=3594,45423 20&hl=en (accessed on May 24, 2015).

Cleveland Daily Herald. 1843–91.

Cleveland Magazine Beer Issue ("Beer Ye, Beer Ye"). Accessed via Great Lakes Publishing website. https://www.clevelandmagazine.com/ME2/dirmod. asp?sid=E73ABD6180B44874871A91F6BA5C249C&type=gen&mod= Core+Pages&gid=2E9CE9E764814174A8030416506764B7 (accessed on May 24, 2015).

Cleveland Plain Dealer. 1845–1991.

Cleveland Scene. "Beer Today, Gone Tomorrow." January 24, 2002. http://www.clevescene.com/cleveland/beer-today-gone-tomorrow/ Content?oid=1478726 (accessed on May 24, 2015).

BIBLIOGRAPHY

Small Business News (Cleveland Edition). "Brewing Up Some Bad News." July 22, 2002. sbnonline.com http://www.sbnonline.com/article/brewing-up-some-bad-news-crooked-river-brewing-co-may-have-produced-some-fine-beer-but-in-this-industry-and-all-others-cash-flow-is-king (accessed on May 24, 2015).

INDEX

INDEX

INDEX

INDEX

R

Red Cap, Carling's 89, 110
Ringneck Brewing Company. *See* Brew
    Kettle, the
Rock Bottom 119
Rocky River Brewing Company 128,
    129, 138, 139
Rose Law 71
Russo, Chris 125, 155

S

saloon(s) 18, 19, 27, 28, 29, 30, 34, 36,
    37, 41, 42, 45, 48, 49, 50, 52,
    55, 61, 62, 63, 67, 70, 74, 75,
    76, 77, 129, 158
Schlather Brewing Company 36, 37,
    55, 56, 118
Schlather, Leonard 23, 33, 35, 36, 37,
    48, 53
Schmidt and Hoffman. *See* Cleveland
    Brewery
Schubert, Dave 144, 145
Seibt, Rick 128
Society of Northern Ohio Brewers
    (SNOBs) 141, 156
soft drinks 38, 45, 56, 64, 66, 75, 76
Spafford, Amos 15, 16
speakeasies 77, 78
Spiesman, Karl 152, 153
Standard Brewing Company 56, 62, 63,
    64, 65, 76, 81, 83, 87, 88, 94, 96,
    97, 101, 103, 105, 106, 120
Star Brewery 51, 53, 56
Sterle's Country House 157
Stoppel Brewery. *See* Columbia
    Brewing Company
Stoppel, Joseph 49
Stumpf, Martin and Michael 29, 33
Sunrise Brewing Company 85, 86, 87

T

temperance 29, 70, 78
Terminal Tower 24, 58, 77

Thirsty Dog Brewing Company 129
tied houses 48
Tip-Top Beer 87, 91
Tremont Taphouse 151, 156
Tveekrem, Andy 117, 141, 142, 144

U

Union Brewing Company 51, 53
Union Terminal. *See* Terminal Tower

V

Van Sweringen family 58, 77
Volstead Act 67, 80

W

Wallaby's 120
Wallace House 16
Walworth Run 19, 50
Welliver, Jerome 122, 124, 132, 133
West Twenty-fifth 34, 49, 63, 113,
    140, 147
Western Reserve Brewing Company
    123, 124, 132, 133
Western Reserve, (Connecticut) 13,
    14, 18
West Side Market 113, 140, 142
Wheeler, Wayne B. 70, 71, 72
Whiskey Island 18, 19, 136
Willoughby Brewing Company 123,
    126, 127, 128
Winking Lizard 156
World Beer Cup 127, 128, 139
World War I 72, 99
World War II 101
Wright, Garin 126, 127, 128
Wright, Robert 126

Y

Yasaki, Shaun 149, 150, 158

ABOUT THE AUTHORS

You could say that Leslie Basalla spends her life immersed in Cleveland craft beer. As co-owner (with her husband, Brian P. McCafferty) of the Cleveland Brew Bus, she spends her weekends escorting groups of imbibers to the city's breweries, guiding them through tastings and relating the stories of each beer and the people who make it. She considers herself an

Photo by Jenna Fournier.

ambassador for both local craft beer and the city of Cleveland. After leaving her career as a newspaper reporter in 2004, Leslie embarked on a series of service industry jobs that, thanks to her knowledge of and passion for craft beer, eventually led her to managing a local brewpub and running its brewhouse tour program. She joined the Brew Bus in 2014 and took over ownership a year later. She is a certified Beer Steward through the Master Brewers Association of the Americas and a certified Beer Server through the Cicerone certification program and is working to gain full Cicerone certification. Her favorite beer styles are saisons and IPAs, and she prefers to drink them outdoors, in the company of her dogs, whenever possible.

ABOUT THE AUTHORS

Peter Chakerian is an award-winning writer, author and journalist whose work has been featured on Yahoo! News, America OnLine, Technorati and RootsRated and in dozens of publications across the country. His twenty-five-year career has earned him several awards, including "Best in Ohio" nods for online journalism by the Ohio Society of Professional Journalists. He is a regular contributor to the *Plain Dealer* and Cleveland.com, covering dining, nightlife, popular culture and entertainment.

Photo by Lindsey Beckwith.

Visit us at
www.historypress.net
....
This title is also available as an e-book